SEEING FOR YOURSELF

SEEING
FOR
YOURSELF

Techniques and Projects for
Beginning Photographers

ROGER GLEASON

CHICAGO
REVIEW
PRESS

Library of Congress Cataloging-in-Publication Data

Gleason, Roger

    Seeing for yourself: techniques and projects for beginning photographers / Roger Gleason.—1st ed.

       p.   cm.

    "A Ziggurat book."

    Includes bibliographical references and index.

    Summary: A hands-on approach to basic photography, with activities and projects that demonstrate technical skills, artistic styles, and creative techniques.

    ISBN 1–55652–159–6 : $14.95

    1. Photography—Juvenile literature.   [1.   Photography.]

I. Title.

TR149.G54 1992

771—dc20   92-18867

                       CIP

                       AC

All photos not otherwise credited are by Roger Gleason.

First edition

Published by Chicago Review Press, Incorporated

814 North Franklin Street

Chicago, Illinois

ISBN 1-55652-160-X

Printed in the United States of America

1 2 3 4 5 6 7 8 9 10

This book is dedicated to the young photographers of the Francis W. Parker School. I am grateful to one in particular, Ms. Cynthia Gordon. With generous recollections she disproved the adage that no one will ever knock at the door and ask if you would like to write a book.

Contents

Preface

I HAVE SPENT more than twenty years helping young students develop their creative powers, and the thrill of watching their vision grow remains happily undiminished.

As a visual arts teacher I play many roles: safety instructor, master of technique, learning coach, historian, and a host of others. But my most important task is to help my students see.

Real vision, both internal and external, fuels the creative engine. There is a certain tension between vision and technique, and technique usually lags behind the ideas that individuals want to express. This is as it should be; mere technique has little to offer.

The purpose of this book is to enhance and refine the act of seeing. I want to encourage beginning photographers to explore an entire range of photographic image-making possibilities. On the following pages I teach the technical essentials through creative projects that define the medium and sharpen the eye. At the end of each chapter I offer a list of valuable references to insure you, the reader/photographer, a continuing, self-guided education.

Most of the projects are illustrated with photographs by young people between the ages of twelve and eighteen. Many of these young photographers are beginners; others have several years of experience. Each has mastered the essentials necessary to realize his or her vision. All have made use of the techniques and projects in *Seeing For Yourself*.

Acknowledgments

MY FIRST AND only flesh-and-blood photo teacher was Mr. Harold Allen of the Art Institute of Chicago. If you have had only one, and it was he, you are fortunate. I am indebted to Mr. Jack Ellison of the Francis W. Parker School, who trusted me to teach photography. To teach, one must learn more; I am most grateful to all those photographers and technicians who have committed their images and their experiences to the printed page.

1 | Setting the Creative Scene

Photo lab essentials include normal room lighting, a safelight, a moveable incandescent light source, plastic chemical and rinsing trays, plastic storage containers, and print-handling tongs.

"God's first creature, which was light."
—Francis Bacon (1561–1626),
English philosopher and essayist

Light is the essence of vision. Photographic vision is part science and as much art as we can manage through careful selection. Each step and phase of photographic work requires the proper lighting.

As we move toward the world of science, our hands reaching for creative tools and our eyes in search of artistic visions, the first step is to create a safe, efficient, and stimulating place to work. For me, the excitement of setting up a darkroom is second only to taking pictures. I've found that a comfortable, well-organized darkroom/studio provides an environment that is both essential and inspiring.

Your Photo Lab

All scientific work requires a laboratory and photography is no exception. Once it is set up, your photo lab will be a place for experiments. Chemicals must be mixed, stored, and spent. Chemical trays, tools, and work-surface must be flexible and easy to clean. You will also need storage space for a wide variety of art materials.

Immediate access to a sink and running water is very useful, but not essential. Your photographs can be transported in a deep tray to a source of running water outside your work area. If these and other conveniences are not contained in one room, then several different areas can serve your needs, depending upon your choice of projects.

Any area where chemicals and light-sensitive materials are used must be well ventilated and accommodate several different lighting situations, including absolute darkness. The trick is to provide good ventilation for a darkroom. Windows and doors must be sealed against light leaks, yet there must be an exchange of air in the work space. Exhaust fans and window air conditioners can provide much of the necessary ventilation.

When you're handling unexposed photographic film, the work space must be absolutely dark. When you're using unexposed photographic paper, the area should be lit solely by a safelight, which allows you to view some light-sensitive materials without spoiling them. Incandescent or fluorescent light will illuminate your lab-studio much of the time. It's easy enough to introduce all these types of lighting into any temporary or permanent work area.

A kitchen or bathroom is usually well equipped with easy-to-clean work surfaces and running water. Problems arise, however, in making such areas light-tight, convenient, and safe from chemical spills. A basement or utility room is usable if it provides good ventilation. Such areas usually afford adequate work space and are relatively easy to darken. This type of space is also more likely to function well as a part-time darkroom and studio.

You can use a table or any stable work surface for your work counter. Cover your counter with plastic drop cloth material for easy cleaning. Your work will inevitably include spills, so you may have to replace the drop cloth from time to time.

Light-Sensitive Materials

Care and concern for proper lighting in your laboratory is essential because light-sensitive material forms the basis for photography. Photographic film and paper are the light-sensitive materials that allow us to produce an infinite variety of images. Film generally is used in cameras to produce translucent negative images (negatives), which are later transferred to photographic paper and referred to as positive prints. In this negative/positive process, one negative can produce an endless number of positive prints.

Paper and film are available for a wide variety of general and special purposes. A confident photographer must proceed to the photo store with enough information to return with the working essentials.

PHOTOGRAPHIC PAPER

Photographic paper is the most useful light-sensitive material for the first group of projects. Photo paper is divided into a number of categories, including color, black and white, fiber-based, resin-coated, and variable contrast paper; it is also divided by grades and textures. Our first paper choices will be confined to paper that produces images in black and white.

The first choice we face is between fiber-based and resin-coated papers. Fiber-based papers are used to produce fine prints and are made of high quality paper coated with light-sensitive emulsion. Fiber-based paper absorbs chemicals during processing and requires long and thorough rinsing during processing. It also takes longer to dry and requires special handling to stay flat.

Resin-coated paper is used for a wide variety of purposes including photographs for reproduction in publications. Light-sensitive emulsion is spread on a resin coated white base. Resin-coated (RC) paper absorbs no chemicals during processing and therefore requires only a short rinsing process. It dries flat and quickly without special handling. Resin-coated paper is an excellent choice for the beginning photographer.

Photographic paper is designed to produce certain levels of contrast between black, white, and gray. High contrast means high levels of black and white and an absence of gray. Lower contrast means more gray content and less black and white.

Papers are manufactured to produce specific grades of contrast (graded) or contrast that varies (variable contrast). Individual types of graded paper are rated according to a numbering system—usually 1 through 5, with 5 indicating high contrast (black and white, no gray) and 1 indicating low contrast (variations of gray, from light to dark, no true black and white). Variable contrast paper offers the possibility of manipulating black, white, and gray content by using a limited range of colored filters. Without the use of filters the paper's contrast is normal, allowing a full range of grays from black to white. Variable contrast paper is the simple way to go, and it offers useful variety in one package of paper.

Another interesting, if increasingly esoteric, distinction between paper types is developing-out paper and printing-out paper. Today, developing-out paper is used almost exclusively; the paper is exposed to light and processed (developed) in chemicals to produce an image. Thus, an image is *developed out* of the paper. Printing-out paper is a much older, slower-acting material that is both exposed and activated by bright light. The image emerges after exposure and can be made permanent using chemicals from the developing-out process. Printing-out paper holds interesting possibilities when electric light is unavailable for making positive prints.

Because the early projects in this book call for black and white photographic paper rather than film, it's important to understand some basic differences between the two materials. Film is generally used in cameras to capture images that exist in a world of color. Whether the film produces images in black and white or color, it must be sensitive to all the colors in the visible spectrum. This means that *all film must be handled in total darkness* when it is manipulated for processing in the studio/darkroom. Later, the image from the film is transferred to photographic paper and is usually referred to as a print.

If you are going to use color paper to produce an image or photograph, remember *color paper must always be handled in total darkness*; it too is sensitive to all the colors in the visual spectrum.

Black and white paper, however, does not need to be sensitive to the entire spectrum of visible light, since the prints are the result of a process that uses negatives that have no color content. Therefore, black and white paper is manufactured so as not to be sensitive to all the colors in the visible spectrum. It is sensitive, primarily, to blue light. Therefore, *black and white paper may be handled under the proper safelight*, one that contains little or no blue light. This allows you to see what you are doing when working with the paper in the studio/darkroom. Darkroom safelights are usually red or orange (amber) colored. Directions that come with your photographic paper provide information concerning the correct safelight color to use.

Advanced photographers will recognize that for many projects film may be used in place of paper. In general, films are more sensitive to light and color. When black and white paper is used in place of black and white film, the resulting images lack subtle gray tones. This is certainly the case when paper is used to make pinhole camera negatives and prints. Beginning photographers, however, will find paper easy to use and will appreciate the technical simplification and time savings that come with paper. I recommend that you use paper for the early projects in this book.

Our paper of choice is a glossy (F), resin-coated (RC) variable contrast paper. If a resin-coated graded paper is selected instead, choose a grade two or three.

The only decisions left are paper size and brand. These choices are usually dictated by project requirements and processing limitations. All paper is manufactured in standard 4 × 5, 8 × 10, 11 × 14, 16 × 20, and 20 × 24 inches.

Each paper manufacturer also provides colored filters used to change the relative contrast of the images produced with the variable contrast paper. The filters of one manufacturer will work on the paper of another. The filters are yellow-orange and varying intensities of magenta. As the filters decrease in yellow-orange intensity and become more intensely magenta, they produce images of increasingly higher contrast. The filters are also numbered 0–5, 0 being the lowest contrast and 5 the highest. Normal or median contrast can be achieved without using any filter. It isn't necessary to purchase contrast filters at first, unless you're planning at the outset to make photographs from film negatives.

Take time to examine paper manufacturers' print samples. You'll notice subtle color differences in both the white and image areas of each paper sample. Some images appear warm brown in tone, others neutral black, and some are cool blue or have a green cast. Choosing paper on the basis of color and tone is usually a matter of personal taste.

I've used many different types and brands of paper over the years, and it's always fun to sample new brands. My choice of paper usually depends on the purpose of the photograph. Proofs, pictures for publication, or photos that accompany written reports are printed on glossy resin-coated stock. Images destined for archives, frames, and wall display are printed on double-weight, fiber-based paper, especially if the prints are large.

I often choose paper as a complement to the subject of a picture. I might choose a warm-toned, textured paper to soften the appearance of an individual's portrait. If I'm printing a landscape I'll use a neutral-toned glossy paper of normal contrast, but for an image of a steel mill or factory I'd be inclined to use a cold-toned glossy paper of high contrast. If I plan to hand-color a picture I usually print it on a matte or pearl surface of medium to high contrast (color is applied more easily to nonglossy paper, and a high contrast image has a better chance to show through transparent color applied by hand).

Photographic Chemicals

Photographic chemistry is the catalyst that allows light to produce and save images on light-sensitive materials. Like all chemicals, photographic solutions should be treated with respect for the work they do, as well as for the dangers they pose.

Just as we protect light-sensitive materials from unwanted light, we must protect ourselves from the unwanted effects of the chemistry necessary to make visible and permanent the images we capture.

You've already tended to the ventilation in your darkroom/studio, so your next consideration should be protective covering to shield your eyes and skin. Much is known about the variety of actual and potential dangers that can accompany the use of photographic chemistry. To this knowledge we should add concern for what remains unknown about the materials we use.

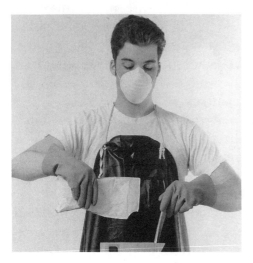 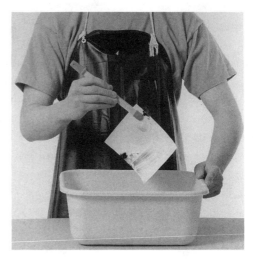

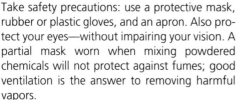

Take safety precautions: use a protective mask, rubber or plastic gloves, and an apron. Also protect your eyes—without impairing your vision. A partial mask worn when mixing powdered chemicals will not protect against fumes; good ventilation is the answer to removing harmful vapors.

When making prints, use gloves whenever possible. (When gloves are not practical, use rubber-tipped tongs.) Large, wet prints are heavy and delicate; use a gloved hand to move them. Keep one hand dry so you can manage tools that must stay chemical-free.

You can easily obtain information about the properties and potential hazards of all chemicals and materials, including substances used for photographic purposes. Directions and warnings for materials appear on packaging and in directions for use. Read the information and warnings thoroughly. *Carefully follow all directions concerning the use and disposal of these products.* A good general rule to follow is not to allow chemicals to touch bare skin or regular clothing.

Most photographic chemicals require mixing or dilution with water or other chemicals. When mixing substances that come in powdered form, wear a particle mask to guard against inhaling airborne chemical dust. Mixing, setup, and cleanup stages require special care for eyes, hands, and clothing. It's advisable to make use of protective gear for eyes and face. Rubber or plastic gloves are also recommended, and a rubber or plastic apron is quite useful. When all the preparation for darkroom work is completed, the normal routine of processing images on paper should be accomplished using print tongs.

Plastic chemical trays are the most useful containers for darkroom work. They're inexpensive, easy to clean, almost unbreakable, and available in sizes that match paper and film. To prevent acquiring too much "stuff," purchase trays that match the largest paper and film size you'll use. If priority is given to the most efficient use of chemicals, always match the size of the tray to the size of paper or film you're using.

At least four trays will be required: one each for three different chemicals and a fourth for rinsing with water. Each tray should be labeled according to chemical type *and used exclusively for that substance.* This is to prevent chemical contamination that might occur if different solutions are inadvertently mixed together.

The same careful material-labeling practices should be used for chemical storage containers. Chemicals can be purchased in amounts to fill a variety of standard volumes: pints, quarts, half-gallons, and gallons. The most useful size is the gallon container. Brown plastic jugs are usually available in photo supply stores. You can also use discarded plastic milk jugs or other similar containers. Some chemicals are affected by light; brown glass or plastic offer special protection. Glass is an excellent storage medium, though breakage is a potential problem. All containers must have caps or stoppers that provide a tight seal. Label each container and note the date that chemicals are mixed so the shelflife of solutions can be accurately calculated. Shelflife and storage information is included in directions that accompany the chemicals.

THE PROCESSING CHEMICALS

Chemicals used to process black and white paper (prints) are simple to use and few in number. Compared to chemicals used in processing color materials, the black and white variety are fairly uncomplicated.

The basic process requires developer, stop bath, and fixer. Since we'll be using a resin-coated paper that absorbs no chemicals, special washing agents will not be required. Projects using film and fiber-based paper make use of a washing agent to help eliminate fixer.

We will make use of developers made expressly for processing paper prints. Developers, for both paper and film, are complex chemical compounds that are carefully formulated to produce certain characteristics. Film and paper require different developers. Most manufacturers of paper and film also produce chemicals for the processing of light-sensitive materials. These chemicals and compounds are similar in formula. Some differences in color and tone are produced with different products that have the same function, but for our initial purposes different brands of paper developer are interchangeable.

Our process requires indicator stop bath. Stop bath is glacial acetic acid and is clear, like water. Indicator stop bath contains an orange-colored dye that turns purple when the stop bath becomes too weak to function, thus "indicating" the need to provide fresh solution. Under a darkroom safelight the exhausted purple stop bath looks dark. It's a good idea to use a light-colored chemical tray to hold the indicator stop bath when processing paper. The remaining chemical is fixer.

Running water is the final ingredient in our black and white paper process. The fourth chemical tray will be used to rinse all traces of the chemicals listed above from the surface of the resin-coated paper. It's a good idea to drill some holes around the rim of the rinsing tray so that prints don't flow over the edge when water is run in the tray; the overflow will exit through the holes and the paper will stay in the tray.

A brief discussion of how photographic chemicals and light-sensitive materials interact is an essential prelude to any of our projects. The photographic process is exactly that, a process, sequential in nature—a process in which there are few shortcuts. Successful projects require a basic understanding of what we can expect from our materials.

When light strikes the emulsion of film or paper, it changes the chemical nature of the light-sensitive elements, in this case, silver halides. The change, however, is not yet visible. The potential, or latent, image will become visible when the film or paper comes in contact with the chemical developer. Upon contact, the unstable silver halides that were struck by light are changed into stable silver. With the change to silver comes instant oxidation. The silver becomes tarnished and the latent image is now visible.

After development is completed, the light-sensitive material is subjected to acid stop bath. The acid bath neutralizes the alkaline developer, thus bringing overall development of paper or film to a complete and consistent halt. Without the use of an acidic bath, development might continue longer in areas where a greater concentration of halides has turned to silver. The goal is even development, and stop bath makes it possible.

The fixer is a silver solvent, a solution that dissolves silver halides quite readily. Given enough time it will also dissolve stable silver. Fixer is used to dissolve the silver salts on film or paper that were not affected by light. A short fixing bath dissolves the silver halides, leaving the stable silver (the image). After the fixing is completed, your paper or film can be exposed to daylight or interior lighting without destroying your image.

If you develop your image and stop the development in acid stop bath and then expose the sensitive material to daylight or normal room lighting without benefit of fixing, all the halide material will turn to stable silver and the film or paper will darken completely, destroying whatever image has formed.

A thorough water rinse is the final step of the process. The purpose of the rinse is to eliminate any trace of processing chemicals, as they will stain the paper and ruin the image if they are not removed.

After chemical processing the prints should be allowed to dry. To aid the drying process and prevent water spots from forming on the prints, it is common practice to squeegee both sides of the print, removing excess water. The print can then be laid flat on a screen or hung on a line with clips. Be careful not to allow the image sides (emulsion) of the prints to come in contact during the drying period. Both resin-coated and paper-based prints will stick together if overlapping is allowed. Let the prints dry for at least half an hour.

Notice that when the prints dry they darken somewhat. This is particularly apparent when a dry print is splashed with a drop of water. The wet area on the image side will show a swelling of the emulsion, which will appear lighter than the surrounding area. As the spot dries it will darken and the swelling will recede.

When prints or film are wet the image, or emulsion side, is very susceptible to scratches and abrasions. Always handle paper and film by the edges and take extra care before they dry.

The following is a list of chemicals in order of use, along with approximate processing times; use the times indicated by the manufacturer. The list contains types of chemicals that are produced by several different manufacturers. All are quite suitable for our purposes.

CHEMICAL	PROCESSING TIME
paper developer	1½ minutes
indicator stop bath	30 seconds
rapid fixer	3 minutes
water rinse	5 minutes

Additional Reading

Photographic Chemistry in Black-and-White and Color Photography by George T. Eaton. Morgan & Morgan, Inc. Publisher, 1988.

Building a Home Darkroom by Ray Miller. The Kodak Workshop Series Publication KW-14, 1981.

Overexposure: Health Hazards in Photography by Susan D. Shaw and Monona Rossol. Allworth Press, 1991.

2 | Images Without Cameras

This photogram of a hand—a photographic negative—is reminiscent of photograms left on cave walls by prehistoric artists. This bold signature image is startling in its timeless graphic immediacy. A positive image is made by placing the negative over unexposed paper and projecting light through it.

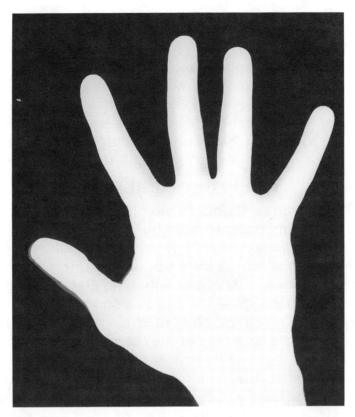

The camera is the great intermediary, a traveling collection box for visual discovery. I take my camera, fancy or plain, out into the city, the open landscape, or the studio. There I select, capture, and store the latent images inside the camera. In the darkroom the latent image is brought forth and projected onto another form of light-sensitive material. I have a picture, a photograph. I find all of this very satisfying, and yet I often want an image that's more direct, more immediate. Fortunately there are ways to do without the great intermediary.

Direct Images

Making our photographic mark can be a very direct experience. Photogram is the most commonly used term to describe the forming of images directly on light-sensitive material. The basic process is simple, and yet making photograms allows us to explore an unlimited variety of immediate imagery—with a high degree of creative control. A simple light source, a sheet of photographic paper, a lineup of chemicals, a safelight in the darkroom, and some everyday objects are all we need.

Once I was asked to create a T-shirt to be used by a school group forming a touch-football team. The big game with the archrival was coming up soon and there was no time for the usual process of taking a picture or making a drawing. Instead I made a photogram using a small football placed on photo paper. On top of the processed image—a white football

15

shape on a black background—I placed a decal of the school's logo. Twenty minutes later the finished image was delivered to a company that produced silk-screened images on T-shirts. The football players had their T-shirts in plenty of time for the big game. There are all kinds of useful applications for the photogram, both artistic and utilitarian.

The Primordial Wow!

With colored safelights providing illumination and chemical trays a secure distance from the white light bulb or flashlight, remove a sheet of light-sensitive material and place the paper flat on the table, glossy side up. Lay one hand down on the paper. With a flashlight or light bulb placed a foot or two above the paper, expose the paper, along with your hand, to the light source for a second or so. Under the glow of the safelight, process the paper under the chemicals using the rubber-tipped tongs.

Seconds after the paper is placed in the developer an image of your hand will begin to emerge. Like the handprint of an early cave artist, the shapes of your very own wrist, palm, and fingers can be somewhat startling in their simplicity. After halting development in the stop bath and fixing the image, place the image in a tray of water and turn on the white light bulb to examine the image.

If you expose your paper to enough light, the image you create will appear a stark black and white. The area of paper covered by your hand will appear white. The uncovered area will appear black or gray, depending on the strength of the light and the length of time the paper was exposed.

The edges of the white image of your hand may appear somewhat darker than the rest, giving the image a glowing effect. The darker edge is the result of light reflecting back and forth from the paper to the rounded edge of your palm and fingers.

It seems obvious that when light strikes the paper and is then chemically processed the covered parts remain white and the exposed parts darken. The dark parts of the image are areas where light strikes the silver salts in the emulsion. The salts turn to silver when contact is made with the chemical developer. The white parts, shielded from the light, continue as unexposed silver salts and wash away with the use of a silver solvent (fixer). The gray areas, if any, are areas where some exposure and some chemical change take place.

THE NEGATIVE-POSITIVE PROCESS

The photographic process allows us to reverse images in terms of light and dark values. The image—a white handprint surrounded by black or dark gray—can be reversed as part of the negative-positive process. Simply put, our first handprint image can act as a photographic negative. Placing this image over an unexposed sheet of photo paper and exposing the two sheets to light will result in an image of reversed values on the newly exposed sheet. The hand will be black or dark gray and the surrounding area will be white or light gray. This is the conventional manner in which negative images are used to produce positive images. The negative's dark areas (the areas around the hand) prevent light from passing through, so those areas on the paper beneath are kept from being exposed and thus remain white.

The white areas (the hand) allow light to pass through to the paper beneath, turning the areas dark. Any image we produce can be reversed in the same manner.

SIMPLE TOOLS

When reversing an image, it's necessary to make certain that the negative is pressed firmly against the unexposed sheet of paper that will become the positive. The simple way is to cover both sheets of paper with a sheet of glass, pressing it down firmly during exposure. If the two sheets of paper are not held firmly together, light will bounce around between them, creating a reverse image that lacks clarity and good transition of opposite values.

Making use of oversized glass and weights will make the process more efficient. The specialized tool for this purpose is a contact printing frame. When a negative is printed by placing it in direct contact with photo paper it is called a contact print. There are various types of printing frames; the oldest and perhaps the best is the wooden version. Its built-in pressure clamps are easy to use and the resulting pressure provides excellent contact.

Save the photogram of your hand—a partial self-portrait—by allowing a 5-minute water rinse. Squeegee both sides on a flat surface and dry it faceup on clean screen mesh or cardboard.

The stark, life-size image of your hand represents a complex shape in silhouette. The immediacy and detail of that image suggests unlimited possibilities for the instant exploration of shape. But we can have much more!

EXPLORING THE POSSIBILITIES

We can explore line and texture. We can produce values from white to black and all the grays in between. We can even have color. We can certainly have image, design, illusion, composition, and juxtaposition. We can, in short, have an unlimited combination of all these exotic elements. We can, as they say, have it all. Anything in this world that can fit on a piece of photographic paper is yours to use for an image.

Exploring the variables of the photographic process provides the best opportunity to make interesting images. The first important variable is exposure. Our light-sensitive material will produce a range of black, white, and gray values that depends upon the intensity of light and the length of time the paper is exposed.

CONTROLLING YOUR MATERIALS

The challenge we face is to control, as much as possible, the amounts of light that our photographic paper is exposed to. We can do this by varying the intensity of light and by varying the length of time the paper is exposed. Controlling both the intensity and the timing is the ultimate goal. By controlling these factors we can regulate light and exercise creative control over the images we produce.

Exposing light-sensitive materials is the special job of cameras and photographic enlargers (see chapter 7). Cameras and enlargers have three primary mechanisms for controlling the amount of light that exposes film and paper: the lens, the aperture, and the shutter; in the case of the enlarger, the timer replaces the shutter.

The camera collects light with its lens; the aperture is an adjustable diaphragm that controls the volume of light that enters; and the shutter is a curtain that opens and closes as needed, controlling the length of time that light can strike film.

The enlarger is a projector used for making photographic prints. It too uses a lens, with an aperture, and a timer that acts as a shutter. Instead of allowing light in, the enlarger projects light, much like a slide projector. Light is projected through film images onto light-sensitive paper.

You don't need a projector to make photographic images on paper, but a photographic enlarger simplifies the business of making photograms.

To make direct images on paper it helps to set up a light source that's just bright enough to allow variation in the timing of exposures, without overexposing our light-sensitive material. We must also devise a simple method to control the timing of exposures.

Photographic enlargers are usually connected to timing devices. Exposure timers can also be used to measure out the exposure of any type of lamp that has a cord and an electrical plug. The most direct method is to time exposures with the second hand of a watch or wall clock. If you don't have such a timing device, you can always count one-one thousand, two-one thousand, etc; it's not terribly scientific, but it works.

SOME USEFUL TESTS

A very useful test to determine exposure control is to place a sheet of photo paper under the intended light source, covering all but a half-inch

Each zone in this test represents 1 second of exposure by incandescent light. The black zone is the darkest value possible, using the minimum amount of exposure. The light source should be adjusted to produce black, gray, and white tones in about 10 exposures (seconds). In this way you can reproduce any single value or the full range by duplicating the timing, light intensity, and distance between the light and the subject.

with black opaque construction paper. Turn on the light for one second. Move the construction paper another half-inch and expose it for another second. Continue this action until all of the paper is exposed, then turn off the light. Process the test paper for the standard times and view it under the white light.

A successful test will provide a graduated range of light gray through black in half-inch strips. If the entire paper is black, use a less powerful bulb and move it farther away from the paper. Experiment with lower wattage bulbs and increase the distance until you achieve a range of values from light gray to black in approximately 6 to 10 seconds of exposure.

If you have difficulty using dimmer bulbs and distance, try placing a sheet of frosted glass or translucent plastic between the light source and the paper. The translucent material will decrease the light striking the paper. It will also diffuse the light and provide for more even illumination of the paper. Moving the light source farther away from the paper also improves the evenness of illumination.

Once you've established a workable exposure system you can begin making images using reliable variable controls. The testing of photographic materials under various lighting situations is an important part of photographic work. A little testing can save a lot of time and material. When conducting tests use fresh chemicals. Old chemistry will not produce reliable results. When testing, avoid using whole sheets of paper; strips of test paper are usually sufficient.

A great deal can be learned about what to expect from materials if we choose a variety of opaque, translucent, and transparent items from which to make direct images. Opaque material will prevent light from striking our paper. These materials will leave the paper white. Translucent material, depending on its density, will allow some light to expose the paper, resulting in various shades of gray. Highly transparent material will allow light to pass unhindered creating black or dark gray areas.

Collect a sampling of objects that transmit varying amounts of light. Hold them up to a light source to get some idea of their opacity and transparency. Arrange them carefully on a sheet of photo paper, taking care not to allow the objects to overlap. Expose the objects on the paper to the minimum amount of light necessary to turn uncovered paper black. We'll use the test results from our value exposure test to determine the exposure time.

Process the paper and examine the image under white light. If we chose objects with a variety of opaque and transparent qualities, we will experience an image that has an interesting range of black, white, and gray values.

Look for items with interesting line quality, shape, and texture. Collecting a group of objects that can be used to produce direct images on paper is the best way to prepare for creative sessions in the studio. As you begin to experiment, you'll discover more about materials and the images they produce.

VALUES AND OVERLAPPING IMAGES

The intentional overlapping of objects used to make photograms is a primary method of creating interesting value changes. The exposure test you conducted earlier represents one form of overlapping. More creative overlapping can be carefully controlled through the exact placement of objects, one over another. Objects scattered in a haphazard manner can achieve a very different effect that relies on chance.

The opaque or transparent quality of the objects that you use will determine the range and character of value changes. Translucent or trans-

The prongs and barbs of a dried teasel plant provide complex shapes for this experiment in creating overlapping images.

parent objects will reveal value changes wherever overlapping occurs. When opaque objects overlap, they simply combine to form a single shape that reveals no overlapping.

Opaque objects can be used to create value changes by moving them around and exposing the paper each time a move is made. To try this method, choose an opaque object, such as a coin, and place it on a sheet of photo paper. Expose it for 1 second. Now move it slightly so that it occupies most of the same area that it covered during the first exposure and expose it for another second. Repeat this action two or three times, taking care not to move the object entirely beyond the boundaries of its first position. Process the paper and view the results. The image should reveal the moves that were made by the object as well as a new set of shapes created by the overlapping.

This overlapping process of moving opaque objects is a form of multiple exposure—the simple result of exposing the paper more than once. Multiple exposures are possible in a number of different photographic situations. With every multiple exposure comes the possibility of overexposing the paper or film. When making use of multiple exposure as an image-making process, gauge your exposures using the value test discussed earlier. Using test results as a guide will help prevent the potential image from becoming overexposed.

Designing with Light

Thus far you have experimented with the intensity and distance of the light source. You have experienced some of the advantages of determining the exact time required to blacken the paper, and you have created timed segments that result in a usable gray scale. You are also familiar with methods of overlapping objects to create and control the formation of black, white, and gray values, and the creation of positive images from negatives.

Now it's time to use your experiments to fully exploit the visual possibilities. The following elements form the universal building blocks of visual invention in all the graphic and sculptural arts: point, line, shape, and volume. Photography not only depends upon these elements, but is uniquely adept at both recording and creating this visual vocabulary.

POINTS OF LIGHT

Points become lines, lines become shapes, shapes turn to volumes, and volumes evolve into complex forms. Our initial goal is to find ways to create a wide variety of point-, line-, shape-, and volume-oriented images. Making direct images on photo-sensitive materials means bringing photographic paper and film into direct contact with source materials.

A single point stays single, but with enough points we can establish a texture. Grains of point-like granules—such as sugar, salt, rice, or sand—can produce as many textures as there are materials. Sprinkle granules directly on photo paper and then draw in the granules. Spread grains over the paper and jiggle it until patterns form. Allow grains to fall onto the paper through the tiny opening of a small container, like sand through the center of an hour glass, drawing in the air as they fall. Carefully sprinkle different size grains over the paper in changing patterns of increasing and decreasing size. Lay some slightly crumpled clear cellophane over a sheet of photo paper and sprinkle grains in random patterns over the plastic; the grains will appear sharp or hazy depending on whether they fall on thin or thick layers of cellophane. The only rule in all of this is to experiment and save your images.

LIGHT LINES

The jump from point to line is easy to conceptualize. The tip of a pencil as it skims a piece of paper, drawing or writing, is an instance of point becoming line. Making line the star of a direct photo image can be wonderfully confusing, given the choices available. You can start with thread or string, coiling and dropping it on paper. Or draw lines on clear cellophane and cover the photo paper with the drawing. Lay wire mesh or hardware cloth over the paper for a grid-like effect. Leaving spaces between opaque or translucent paper laid over light-sensitive materials will yield a line of varying thickness. Or try placing an abandoned spider web onto photo paper and exposing it.

THE SHAPE OF SHADOWS

A shape is formed when line encloses a space. Searching for natural lines that lead to shapes is as easy as searching the ground we walk on for fallen leaves and other plant forms. The veins of a leaf or the shapes of flowering plants offer an intriguing array of delicate forms. When pressed into service, light can produce an X-ray effect in our natural forms that appears to illuminate the very structure and design of the natural world around us.

With an entire world of natural and man-made points, lines, textures, and shapes to incorporate in our visual experiments, the challenge is to design a world of our own. Seeing familiar forms in a strikingly different light allows us to reshape parts of the world around us. By taking our cues from nature we can turn our observations and discoveries into visual statements.

Aside from the design problems inherent in fusing the geometric and organic, interesting symbolism begins to emerge. Using geometric and organic shape together becomes a metaphor for the structures of humanity and our relationship with nature.

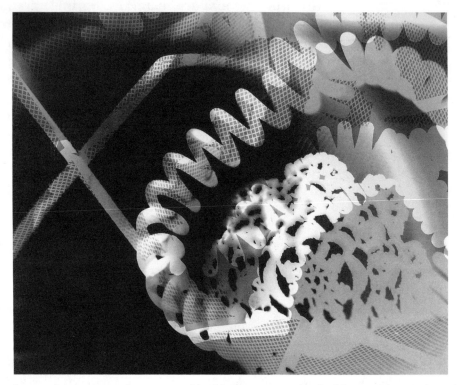

Point, line, and shape are well represented in this photogram of a flexible extension cord, cooking utensils, and a lace doily. A light source was directed at three different arrangements of the objects placed on the paper. The direction of the light changed with each arrangement.

The Art of Juxtaposition

While the stark black and white of the direct image provides a world of striking silhouettes, a full pallet of subtle grays that bridge the gap between extreme black and white offers to fill in all the gaps.

The startling image is often based upon a pairing of the unlikely. The art of juxtaposition brings together elements and images that produce the unexpected; visions one might expect to see only in the world of dreams. The unexpected juxtaposition of images is the basis for Surrealist and Dadaist art, which continue to confront conventional thought.

Combining photogram and photographic images is also accomplished by cutting images apart and reordering them, or by combining them with different images to create a photo montage or photo collage.

The photo montage is made up of pieced-together photo images. A strictly photographic look can be maintained by using processed photo paper as a background. The paper can simply be placed in fixer and rinsed so that it will remain white, exposed to the point where it turns black and is processed like any image, or exposed and processed to provide a gray tone somewhere in between.

The white edges of the photographs and photograms that have been cut or trimmed can be disconcerting when adhered to darker images or backgrounds. They can ruin any illusion of shared space and surface between images. Coloring the edges of cut-out shapes with gray or black markers can eliminate telltale edges and restore the illusion of shared space and surface. (Use colored markers for colored images.)

You can form a collage from any collection of flat material, including decorative paper of every sort, drawings, magazine and newspaper pages, office copier reproductions, and actual photographs.

Juxtaposition of images using the techniques of photo montage and collage opens a world of image-making possibilities for the photographer, painter, filmmaker—for anyone interested in visual invention.

There are times when photographers feel that every possible subject has already been thoroughly explored. But then we go to a gallery or open a book and see photographs, drawings, or paintings that seem fresh and original. At times like that I experience a great sense of satisfaction. I'm reminded that the possibilities for choosing, creating, and combining images are infinite.

The best part is that while you and I may take our images seriously, our method is based on play. Playing with all the possibilities, playing with our eyes and minds wide open. Some may call it experimentation, others refer to it as research and development; for you and me it's playfulness of the highest order.

Additional Reading

The History of Photography by Beaumont Newhall. The Museum of Modern Art, New York, 1964.

3 | Building Pinhole Cameras

Tools for building cardboard pinhole cameras include a metal T-square and angle, utility knife, hobby knife, ¼-inch hole punch, push pin, pencil, aluminum foil, and black photographic masking tape.

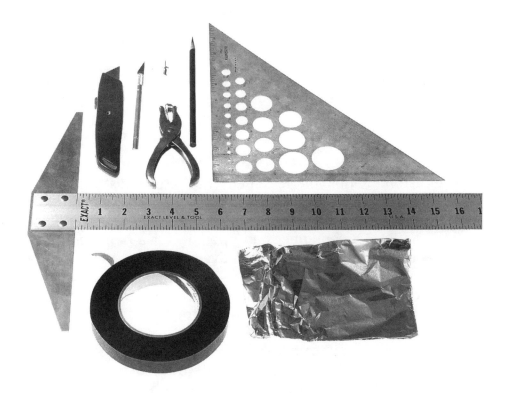

U sing little more than a box and a pin you can provide yourself with a working camera. With the light-sensitive materials we use to make photograms, we can load a pinhole camera and take clear pictures that display unique photographic qualities.

Pinhole cameras can take on all shapes and sizes. Some are custom made, others are adapted for camera work from ready-made containers. Depending on their geometric shape and volume they can produce images with distinctly different qualities. Rectangular containers generate images relatively free of distortion. Curved containers produce pictures with useful and dramatic distortions.

Essential requirements for all cameras, including the pinhole variety, are a sturdy enclosed volume that opens and closes easily, a nonreflective black interior, and a light-tight seal on all seams and openings.

ESSENTIAL TOOLS FOR THE CONSTRUCTION OF PINHOLE CAMERAS

- metal ruler (for measuring and cutting)
- utility or hobby knife
- bulletin board push pin, needle, or straight pin
- pencil

OTHER USEFUL TOOLS

- metal T-square
- 90–45-degree metal drafting angle
- hole punch

The Custom 57

The custom-made pinhole camera that records distortion-free visual perspective, while allowing full use of light-sensitive materials, requires the construction of a simple rectangular box and lid. The box needs an opening for a pinhole at one end and a slot to hold light-sensitive material at the opposite end.

The camera's customized dimensions are determined by the proportions of our choice of photographic film or paper. In the following examples you will use photographic paper and customize your camera's dimensions to match standard 5 × 7–inch resin-coated stock, thus the title *Custom* 57. Paper and film of this format will produce pinhole images large enough for easy viewing and small enough for convenient handling and modest budgets.

CONSTRUCTION MATERIALS REQUIRED FOR YOUR CUSTOM 57

- sheet of dull black mat board
- roll of black photographic masking tape
- a few square inches of aluminum foil

Step 1: establish the dimensions of the camera.

You want your camera box to fit your 5 × 7–inch paper, therefore you already know two out of three necessary dimensions. The interior will measure 5 inches high and 7 inches wide. Since the pinhole of your camera is circular it will form a circular image like the pattern of a flashlight. All your photo paper should fit within the image circle. To make sure this happens, measure the diagonal of the photo paper and use this dimension (8½ inches) to establish the length of your camera: the distance from pinhole to photo paper.

Step 2: plan the basic camera box.

The key to building a functional camera box is to take into consideration the fact that the five sides (the lid will form the

The Custom 57 pinhole camera is a cardboard box with interior dimensions that allow the use of a full sheet of photo paper or film (5 3 7 inches). This style of pinhole camera produces images with little or no distortion.

sixth side) will overlap; overlapping must be designed so that you are left with your original interior dimensions of 5 × 7 × 8½ inches. The thickness of the overlapping cardboard will determine the outside dimensions.

Step 3: lay out the sides and bottom of the box.

Using the straight edge ruler, or T-square and angle, measure and draw the outlines of the sides and bottom on the white side of the cardboard. Use a sheet of 5 × 7 photo paper and a sample thickness cardboard as a measuring guide.

Step 4: cut out the sides and bottom.

Use the straight edge to score each cut lightly; don't try to cut through the board in one pass. A strip or two of black masking tape on the underside of your straight edge will help prevent it from slipping.

Step 5: prepare the front of the box for the pinhole.

You will use aluminum foil to make the camera's pinhole. Position the pinhole on the camera's front side, in the very center. If you draw diagonals on one of the 5 × 7 sides, the resulting X will mark the spot. Cut out a small rectangle around the center and cut or punch a hole in the center of the X; this cutout, with its punched hole, is the target for the eventual pinhole. Set the cutout aside.

Step 6: assemble the box.

Using the opaque black masking tape, carefully attach the front, back, and sides. Make certain that the black side of the board forms the interior of the box. At first the tape should be used only on the outside of the box. When the four sides are attached, place the unit over the layout of the box bottom, matching the outside corners to the drawing. If no adjustments are required, cut out the bottom and attach it to the sides with tape.

Step 7: make the lid.

The lid of your box must fit snugly—but not too snugly. It must keep out light but open and close easily. These requirements can be met by making another shallow box to fit over the open top of the one you have just completed.

Determine the depth of the lid by measuring the distance from the top of the pinhole cutout to the top edge on the main box. This distance represents the maximum depth the lid can be without blocking the actual pinhole once the hole and lid are in place. Cut four long strips the width of this dimension to form the sides of the lid. Using the main box as the guide, fit the side pieces of the lid.

The top area of the lid can be determined by placing the taped sides of the lid over the remaining cardboard, squaring up the corners, and tracing the outside edge onto the box to be covered. Cut and assemble. Place the new lid on the main box. Loose is better than tight; you can always pad the inner sides of the lid with extra tape.

Step 8: make the paper/film holder.

Strips of black cardboard, taped to each interior side at the back of the camera, will form a channel to hold light-sensitive material. Leave just enough space between the strips and the back to slide photo paper firmly in place.

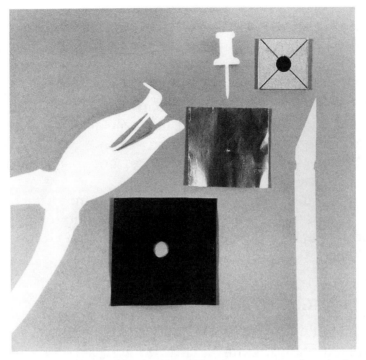

The same pinhole structure is used for all cardboard cameras. Metal or plastic cameras make use of the foil square and black tape cover. Each square of material, beginning with the cardboard cutout (cardboard, foil, black tape) is cut successively larger, with the larger black tape square on the outside. The foil and tape will seal cuts made in the cardboard camera.

Step 9: make the pinhole.

Smooth out a square inch of aluminum foil over a piece of scrap cardboard. Carefully pierce the center of the foil with just the tip of the pin. The pinpoint should pass through the foil, penetrating but not making a hole in the cardboard below. Without bending the square of foil, carefully inspect the pinhole, checking to see that it is both round and flat.

Step 10: install the pinhole.

Punch a hole in the center of a square of black masking tape. Carefully place the punched hole in the tape over the foil hole to form a bull's eye. Now tape the foil pinhole in the center of the cutout that you removed from the camera in step 5. Tape the cutout back into the camera front, black side facing in. Your Custom 57 is now complete.

The Wide-Angle Pinhole

Pinhole cameras that provide a wide-angle view can be custom-built or adapted from ready-made containers. With a few simple additions and modifications, you can make your version from a long cylindrical cardboard box.

The cylindrical sides of the box will distort the pinhole image, giving the same effect as an extreme wide-angle lens: straight lines will curve and distances between objects will appear greatly exaggerated.

To adapt the cylindrical box for use as a camera we need to paint interior surfaces black, create the opening for a pinhole, and add a flat base so the cylinder can be laid on its side without rolling.

ESSENTIAL TOOLS FOR THE CONSTRUCTION OF A WIDE-ANGLE PINHOLE CAMERA

- metal ruler (for measuring and cutting)
- utility or hobby knife
- bulletin board push pin, needle, or straight pin
- pencil

The wide-angle pinhole camera is made from a cylindrical cereal box with a cardboard top reinforced with tape. Painting the camera protects it from moisture, and a block of wood is fastened to one side so the camera can be used in either a vertical or horizontal position. By adding a teenut to the bottom of the wooden block you can mount the camera on a tripod.

- a few square inches of aluminum foil
- hole punch
- opaque black masking tape
- flat black latex or polymer paint
- piece of pine, 1 × 4 × 12 inches

Step 1: choose the right size box and handle with care.

The circumference of the container should be roughly double that of the shorter edge of the paper. This ratio will insure that adequate tension will hold the paper firmly in a curved position, matching that of the container. Find a container that will provide a very usable volume for 5 × 7 paper. (The paper may require trimming to fit properly.) If the container is new and unopened, take care to open it carefully so as not to damage the all-important lid.

Step 2: paint the interior surfaces flat (mat) black.

Wipe the insides of the container and lid free of dust. Paint the interior surfaces of both container and lid with flat black latex or polymer paint. Allow the paint to dry for at least one hour.

Step 3: prepare an opening for the pinhole.

The aluminum foil pinhole will be centered on the length of the cylinder between the flat ends. Locate that center point and mark it with a pencil. Draw a square inch around it so that each side of the square is 1/2 inch from the center mark. Cut through three sides of the square, forming a trap door; the uncut hinge of the door should lie on the flat, not the curve. Fold out the trap door and punch a hole in the center of the X; our foil pinhole will be placed in the center of the punched cardboard hole.

Step 4: make the pinhole.

Smooth out a square inch of aluminum foil over a piece of scrap cardboard. Carefully pierce the center of the foil with just the tip of the pin. The pinpoint should pass through the foil, penetrating the cardboard below. Without bending the square of foil, carefully inspect the pinhole, checking to see that it is both round and flat.

Step 5: install the pinhole.

Punch a ¼–inch hole in the center of a square of black masking tape. Carefully place the punched hole in the tape over the foil pinhole to form a bull's eye. Now tape the foil pinhole in the exact center of the punched cardboard hole in the trapdoor (step 3). Push the trapdoor back in place and seal the cuts with additional masking tape.

Step 6: reinforce and seal the camera lid.

The lid to the container needs to be reinforced with tape. Some container lids are made of translucent plastic; a layer of tape on the end and sides insures that the lid will be opaque as well as strong. Place the lid in position on the camera when applying the tape to prevent the lid from being stretched into an oval.

Step 7: attach the wood base.

You want to be able to steady your wide-angle camera in both a vertical and horizontal position. Therefore, one end of the 1 × 4–inch pine base should be trimmed flush with the closed end of the cylinder container. This will allow the camera to rest firmly on end. The opposite end of the base will extend to the lid without interfering with its operation. With the camera lid in place, tape the base firmly to the container, front and back.

The container and wood base should be positioned such that when the camera is in the horizontal position the pinhole is aimed upward approximately five degrees. Now you can use your wide-angle pinhole camera.

The Pinhole 360

The *Pinhole 360* provides the ultimate wide-angle: 360 degrees of relatively uninterrupted image. Quite naturally, the required container is circular. A round cookie or candy box of metal or cardboard is ideal, or try to find an old-fashioned hat or cheese box.

Multiple pinholes of similar diameter are a challenging requirement in producing an image in-the-round. So too, is forming the essential island of circular paper at the camera's core. Image overlap and gaps are characteristics of complete circular pictures. You can minimize these characteristics by varying the number of pinholes and altering the circumference of the paper core. It's good to experiment. Keep flexibility in mind as you construct such a camera.

The Pinhole 360 is made from a tin cookie box. Four 1/4-inch holes are drilled in the sides 90 degrees apart and centered from top to bottom. Lift the lid and you find a cylindrical core of tin or cardboard half the circumference of the cookie box (see diagram of top and side view). Our light-sensitive paper is looped around this core. The notched strip of black paper (shutter) that surrounds the outside of the camera is designed to allow the photographer to open and close all four pinholes at once.

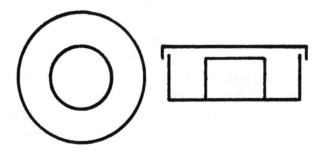

The diagram shows the interior construction of the Pinhole 360. The left side displays a top view of the open tin cookie box. The inner circle represents the added paper core. The right side of the diagram displays a side view, with the camera lid on top and the cookie tin, with paper core, below.

As with other pinhole cameras, it's a good idea to think in terms of paper size when deciding the camera's overall dimensions. A larger paper size, such as 11 × 14–inch material, cut into strips, may offer the greatest convenience. The trick is to design an easy-to-load paper-holding system that firmly supports a single, cylindrical strip of paper at the camera's center. The circumference of the paper strip will be slightly greater than that of the paper support core.

ESSENTIAL TOOLS FOR THE CONSTRUCTION OF A 360-DEGREE PINHOLE CAMERA

- metal ruler (for measuring and cutting)
- utility or hobby knife
- bulletin board push pin, needle, or straight pin
- pencil
- a few square inches of aluminum foil
- metal hole punch or drill
- opaque black masking tape
- flat black paint—latex for cardboard, enamel for metal
- piece of opaque black construction paper

Step 1: determine camera and paper size.

Begin by cutting a narrow strip from the long edge of the paper size you would like to use. Form the strip into a continuous loop and tape the butted ends together. This loop represents the size of the central, paper-holding core of the camera. The actual size of the core should be slightly smaller than the loop so you can place the paper down over the core with ease.

The ideal size of the outer circle, or camera container, is a circle twice as large as the paper core. To say it another way, the radius of the paper-holding core should be half that of the outer wall of the container. This size relationship between the inner and outer circle is important so that the image will be adequately covered when the paper is exposed to four equally spaced pinholes. It will also provide for a minimum of image overlap.

Find a container that comes close to the dimensions established when you form the paper loop. You can trim the paper to accommodate a useful container that comes close to the ideal size. (It may be necessary to use a larger paper size than originally planned.)

Step 2: place the pinholes.

To strike a balance between potential gaps in the image and too much overlapping, use at least four pinholes, one at each 90-degree point of the compass. Find the vertical center of the container and mark it along the container's circumference. Along the centered circumference mark the 90-degree divisions. Carefully punch or drill holes where the 90-degree marks intersect the centered circumference. These holes will accommodate the actual foil pinholes, which will be added later.

Step 3: construct the paper core.

Calculate the half-radius core size for the camera container and find or make a sturdy cylinder to form the core. Rather than attach the core to the actual bottom of the camera, fasten the core cylinder, using black tape, to a black cardboard circle cut to match the camera's bottom. Make certain that the core, with its circular cardboard base, is the same height as the sides of the container. Check to see that the lid can be closed tightly when the core is in place.

Step 4: paint all interior surfaces of the camera.

If the camera container is metal, spray or brush the surface with flat black enamel or rust-resistant paint. If camera construction is of cardboard, use flat black latex or polymer paint. Paint the inside of the container, the core structure, and the inside surface of the lid. When all parts are dry, place the paper core and its base inside the camera.

Step 5: build a shutter device.

The shutter is a band of opaque black construction paper with slots cut to align with the camera's pinholes. The band fits around the full height of the camera's outside surface and is loose enough to slide freely from side to side. The idea is to allow light to pass through the pinholes by twisting the band until the pinholes and slots align. Moving the shutter band left or right will close off light to the pinhole, thus all four pinholes can be opened or closed at once. Wrap the band around the camera and tape lightly. Mark the position of the pinholes from inside, unfasten the band, cut slots slightly larger than the pinholes and replace the band.

Step 6: construct and install the pinholes

Produce and install the pinholes as in the earlier camera models, taking special care to make four pinholes that are as similar in size as possible. Place the tape and aluminum foil holes over the holes punched in the side of the camera. When the pinholes are installed the camera is ready for use.

Refining Your Pinhole Camera

All pinhole cameras can be refined by adding additional components and redesigning others. Once you're familiar with the picture-taking process and all its variables, you'll discover ways to make improvements. You may even choose to design your own camera. Pinhole models can be made to produce images as small or as large as you can manage. Parts can be added to mount your camera on a tripod, or you can build your own tripod. The variations in design and materials are endless.

Why Does It Work?

Why does the pinhole camera work? The key, of course is the pinhole, known also as an *aperture*. In a regular camera the aperture, along with a lens and shutter, are all adjustable controllers of light (see chapter 6). The aperture governs the *volume* of light that enters the camera at any given time. The pinhole, much smaller than a normal aperture, allows so little light to enter the camera that all of it is focused on the film or paper. With the pinhole camera, it is necessary to control only the length of exposure.

What goes on inside the pinhole camera? As with any camera, particles of reflected light streak through the aperture from the world out front, striking the light-sensitive material at the back. Many particles are then reflected off the film or paper and absorbed by the dull black coating of the camera's interior. The light particles hitting the film or paper have left a latent image that will emerge when processing takes place.

Historical Byte

The image-forming capabilities of the pinhole have been known for centuries. We can only imagine the first time that bright light filtered into a darkened room or a tent though a tiny opening, offering images of the world outside.

The recorded history of art and early photography are filled with descriptions of image-collecting devices driven by pinhole-inspired technology such as the *camera obscura* and the *camera lucida.* These early devices were enhanced by the addition of lenses.

The simple pinhole projector, used to safely view phenomenon like a solar eclipse of the sun, is a perfect example of pure pinhole technology in common use today.

Additional Reading

The Keepers of Light by William Crawford. Morgan & Morgan, 1979.

Art and Photography by Aaron Scharf. Penguin Books, 1986.

Photographic Materials and Processes by Stroebel, Compton, Current, and Zakia. Focal Press, 1986.

4 | Taking Pinhole Camera Pictures

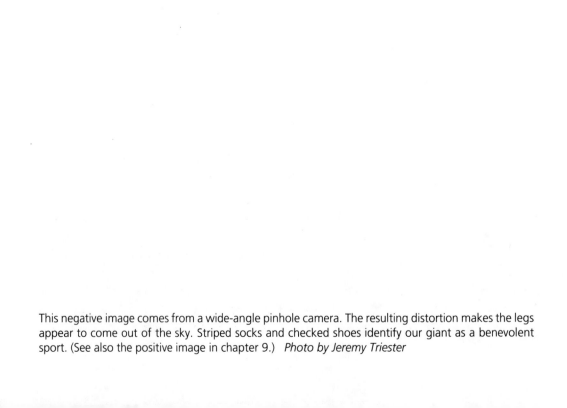

This negative image comes from a wide-angle pinhole camera. The resulting distortion makes the legs appear to come out of the sky. Striped socks and checked shoes identify our giant as a benevolent sport. (See also the positive image in chapter 9.) *Photo by Jeremy Triester*

Y ou should prepare the darkroom to make pinhole photos the same way you set up to make photograms. Your work area should be well ventilated and lit by safelights, your chemical trays filled, and your print tongs ready.

Preparations for Picture Taking

As you set about using your pinhole camera you should have paper or cloth towels handy. Your hands must be dry and free of chemicals, since you will continually return to your box of photo paper.

Load your camera under safe light conditions. Remember, paper is manufactured so as not to be sensitive to certain colors of light, such as red or amber. Panchromatic film, the type most commonly used, is sensitive to all colors of visible light. If you are using film instead of paper, you must load and process the film in absolute darkness. Also, you must use a developer that is formulated for film rather than paper.

Loading a pinhole camera requires great care in handling the light-sensitive material. You should make every effort to handle the material by its edges. An errant fingerprint, especially on the glossy emulsion side of the paper, may leave a permanent mark. Staining can also occur if hands are not free of photo chemicals.

The photographic paper should be trimmed to fit, if necessary, using a small paper cutter or scissors. If several people are working together, names or initials can be written, in pencil, on the back (the dull side) of the paper. Be certain to place any writing on the very edges of the sheet.

The paper or film should be loaded into the camera on the side opposite the pinhole, with the glossy emulsion side facing the pinhole. If your camera is cylindrical make sure the paper is pushed into place at the bottom of the cylinder, as well as the top.

Testing Your Camera

Before you go to the trouble of making pictures you must check to see if there are any leaks in the camera. Load the camera with paper, marking an X on the sheet at the edge that is near the lid. This time, carefully tape over the pinhole with opaque photo tape, being careful to place a bit of paper between the tape and the pinhole to prevent the tape from sticking to the foil.

Bring the camera outdoors and set it in the midst of the brightest light possible and leave it there for a full minute. During the 1-minute leak test, move the camera around so that all sides are hit by the bright light.

Return to the darkroom and process the paper as though it had been exposed for a picture. If there is a leak the paper will darken. If the paper darkens at one end or in one corner, you will be able to find the general location of the leak by checking it against the X that you marked on the paper. Putting some extra tape over a seam or lining the lid will usually seal the leak.

With the paper loaded, firmly secure the camera lid all around. Cover your paper box and place your finger over the pinhole of your camera. You may now leave the safelit darkroom and venture outdoors to take a picture.

Survey the immediate area and find an object or scene that interests you. Protect the camera from blowing winds and avoid aiming the pinhole directly into the sun. If possible, select a scene that includes moving objects as well as stationary ones. Seeing what happens to objects that move during an exposure will prove interesting.

Set the camera down on firm ground (holding the camera during exposure will produce a blurry image), all the while keeping a finger over the pinhole. Aim the pinhole in the general direction of your subject. The subject should be lit by bright sunlight. When your aim is set, gently uncover the pinhole so as not to move the camera; allow light to enter the pinhole for 30 seconds. As the exposure time draws to a close, approach the camera carefully and gently cover the pinhole. Now, it's back to the darkroom (and the protective illumination of safelights).

Your first pinhole pictures will be very telling. Is your pinhole the right size and well formed? Is it aimed straight ahead? Your first few images will answer these questions.

Troubleshooting

Back inside the safelit darkroom you can open the camera and remove the paper, handling it as much as possible by its edges. Process the paper just as you did your photograms: 1½ minutes in developer, 10 seconds in stop bath, and 1 minute in fixer. Use tongs to move the prints and agitate each tray gently throughout the sequence. Remove the image from the fix and place it in the rinse tray.

It's difficult to accurately observe the results under safelight; turn on the white work light to judge the final results.

If a clear image has formed, it will appear strange: what you thought would be light will be dark and vice versa. What you have, of course, is a negative image. A bright sky will appear black and a dark shadow will appear white. Later you can use the negative to produce a positive image, just as you did with photograms.

You may also notice that the image is darker at the center and lighter as it approaches the edges. This is the result of not having a lens in front of the aperture. One function of a lens is to distribute light evenly from center to edge and from edge to edge. Later you will learn ways to even up this uneven distribution of light.

If your image is barely dark enough to see, it is underexposed. You will need to increase exposures by at least two or three times. Reload the camera, return to the same scene, and make a new, longer exposure.

Determine whether or not the light level has changed. Has the sun gone behind a cloud? Has the area been overtaken by shadows? If no apparent lighting changes have occurred, take a new picture and make a note of the new exposure time.

You want a negative that has a full range of black, white, and gray values. When this has been achieved, record the results so that the next time you take a picture under similar lighting conditions you can achieve correct exposure without guessing.

If your first exposure is too dark, return to the same scene with a new sheet of paper loaded in the camera and expose the paper for one-half the duration of the first exposure (15 seconds). Process the paper and evaluate the results. If the image remains too dark, try the same scene again for half the time (7 seconds). If the image remains too dark again, you need a new, smaller pinhole. When the new pinhole is installed, redo the tests until a proper exposure is made and record the results.

It may be that your camera is producing reasonably good images with very short (3–10 second) exposures. If, however, the images are not sharp, particularly in areas that depict stationary objects at a distance of 10 feet or more, a change of pinhole is warranted. A smaller pinhole will produce sharper images, even though exposure time will increase.

Your initial goal is to record successful exposures made under a variety of lighting conditions: bright sunlight, bright-hazy conditions, overcast—the usual gamut of outdoor conditions. Record the results and attach them to the camera.

Adhesive labels are handy for attaching exposure records to your camera. You can always update the information by sticking a new label over the old one. Remember, if you change the pinhole, you change its size. This means that the volume of light allowed into the camera will also change; therefore you must make new exposure tests.

Aside from over and underexposures, other aberrations may appear in your pictures. Here are a number of possible glitches you can expect, along with some troubleshooting tips to help avoid problems.

VIGNETTING

If part of your image is always cut off or unexposed, it means that the foil pinhole is poorly centered over the punched cardboard hole in the camera body. If the pinhole is too close to the punched cardboard, a curved section of the image will be blocked. The pinhole must be removed and recentered.

DISTORTION

If you're using a pinhole camera of cylindrical design and the paper is loaded against a curved surface, your images will appear distorted, just as they would if you used a regular camera with a very wide-angle lens. This distortion is normal, and it provides a wide angle of view and the appearance of greater distance between objects.

FLARE

If images from your cylindrical camera show a dark, horizontal line across the center portion of the negative, it means that the angle of the sun and the tilt of the camera caused light to reflect from the bottom edge of the paper to the center of the picture. This generally happens when photographing at midday when the sun is high and bright.

SUN STREAKS

If a black line meanders over part of a negative image, it means that at some time during picture taking, the camera was pointed directly at the sun. Dark streaks mean that direct sunlight entered the camera at an angle during exposure.

Occasionally the dark streaks and lines are interesting; more often, they are not desirable additions to the image.

FAINT IMAGE

Some aberrations that appear may be the result of chemical processing errors. The developer may be too cold—well below the recommended 68 degrees F (warm the solution). The developer may be worn out (use fresh solution).

PARTIALLY DEVELOPED IMAGE

Make certain that the entire negative is immersed in the processing solutions.

UNEVEN DEVELOPMENT

The negative has been removed from the developer too soon, or it may not have been agitated enough. Process a newly exposed image for the full amount of time and agitate constantly.

Traveling

Like any camera, your pinhole version can travel. Staying close to your darkroom during photographic sessions has the advantage of allowing quick image processing, but once you've mastered the basics of judging exposure, venture farther from the lab. This will require some additional preparations, but the photographic opportunities will more than make up for the extra effort!

A photographer's changing bag is a portable dark enclosure. You can use it to load and unload paper and film when you're in the field. The changing bag looks like a shirt with a zippered end and two arm holes ringed with elastic. The zippered end opens, revealing a second bag within, also zippered.

The idea is to place light-sensitive materials, cameras, or film holders inside the bag and close both zippers. Place both hands inside the bag through the arm-like openings. The elastic ends will hug your arms, preventing light from entering the bag, while you use the bag just as you would your blackened darkroom.

Traveling pinhole photography requires a container for unexposed paper and another one to hold exposed paper. You can take a series of pinhole pictures by doing your usual camera loading and unloading in the sealed changing bag. You can place exposed images in the second light-tight paper box and process them when you return to your darkroom.

Making Positive Pinhole Prints

Once you've exposed your paper and processed the negative images, it's time to make positive prints. The best method is to make use of the contact printing frame. In the absence of a frame, use a sheet of glass with weights. As with the photograms, you can place your dry negative over a new sheet of paper and expose the negative to light.

If you're using a printing frame, place the negative on the glass faceup. Make certain that the negative is completely dry. Place a fresh sheet of paper over the negative, emulsion side down (glossy side down), and lock the back of the frame over both sheets. Turn the frame over and expose the new paper through the negative. When the exposure is completed, turn the frame over, open the back, remove the newly exposed paper, and process it through the chemicals just as we did with the photograms.

Making positive images is much like exposing film in your camera: the more light that passes through the negative, the darker the positive will be. A negative that looks really dark will require a lot of light to produce a proper positive print. A negative that is mostly white, or light gray, will not take as long to expose. After a while you'll become quite adept at judging the necessary exposure time to produce a good print. Essentially, you want to reproduce the same good black, white, and gray tones found in the negative.

If the image on the negative is too dark or too faint, you probably won't get a good print. Your time will be well spent if you concentrate on achieving good exposure in the negative. Trying to extract a good print from a poor negative is a lost cause.

Without a lens negative images display a darker center and fade toward the edges. When you make a positive print, you can correct a good deal of this uneven distribution of light. By exposing the negative in a way that concentrates more light at the center of the image, you can produce a positive print that appears fairly even.

Using more black construction paper punch a hole in the center of a sheet that's cut a bit larger than your photo paper. The idea is to make your normal exposure and then expose more light through the hole in the construction paper. We can aim the light at the center of the negative. By moving the paper back and forth, closer, then farther away, we can spotlight the center of the image, in radiating patterns. This action will expose the center of the negative more than the edges and will result in a positive image that appears more evenly exposed. The process of adding additional light to part of a print is called burning, or burning in.

You can, if you choose, alter the light and dark areas of a print by dodging, or withholding light from part of a negative as you expose to produce a positive print. Rather than using a hole in a black sheet of paper, you can use a small circle of black paper—or any shape you choose—attached to a wire handle. During exposure, attempt to withhold light from areas that you would like to keep from becoming too dark in the positive print. During exposure, insert the cut shape between the print and the light source. As the exposure is taking place, jiggle the wire so that a definite shadow does not form on your print; this would look unnatural. When burning and dodging, always jiggle your tool of choice to create a gradual change from light to dark.

When burning and dodging pinhole images, it is very helpful to lightly trace the essential parts of an image on the back of the negative as an aid to locating areas to be burned or dodged.

The negative-positive process allows us to print as many positives as we want from a single negative. The printing process allows us to make our print lighter or darker than our original scene and, if we choose, improve the uneven light quality inherent in pinhole images. We can darken or lighten images to create changes in feeling and mood. We can burn or dodge areas of the picture to obscure or highlight particular parts of an image. Much of the art in photography occurs in the process of changing a negative image into a positive print.

Historical Byte

Photographing with pinhole cameras offers insight into the working methods of early photographers. From the early 1850s to the late 1880s large, simple, tripod-bound cameras and cumbersome processing methods made early photography a physically demanding process. Light-sensitive materials were slow to react to light, making exposure times long and stop action impossible. In the late 1880s improvements in light-sensitive materials and processing made possible the introduction of increasingly smaller hand-held cameras. The increased sensitivity, and smaller size of film and plates, allowed camera shutters to open and close fast enough to stop action and forgo tripods. Smaller cameras required smaller, easier to handle film formats.

View Camera Users

Use a view camera, with its film holders, as a pinhole camera. Just remove the front and back lens elements from the shutter and replace them with a pinhole. You can even use instant film and film backs.

Additional Reading

The International Pinhole Photography Exhibition Catalog, essays by James Hugunin and Eric Renner. Center for Contemporary Arts of Sante Fe, 1989.

5 | Pinhole Camera Projects

The foot of the brick column on the left is standing firm against the leaning wall on the right. A double exposure made with a wide-angle pinhole camera makes the distortion possible. The first image—a brick wall up close—is overlapped by a side view of a young woman's lower leg, with a building in the background. The bright sky in the second exposure wipes away most of the brick wall.
Photo by Jennifer Wallack

Your pinhole camera is capable of technical feats that surpass even the most complicated and expensive camera systems. Aspects of pinhole operation that at first seem backward soon offer valuable insights into the nature and history of photographic practice.

Low-Tech Pinhole Powerhouse

The exclusive ability to render nearly complete depth of field—to record images that maintain sharpness from several inches away to infinity—is the singular technical advantage of the pinhole camera. In a high-tech world hungry for unusual and dramatic images, this is no small accomplishment.

The small pinhole—a fixed aperture—allows a small volume of light to enter the camera over a prolonged period of time, so stopping action is something of an impossibility. In many situations, exposures are so long that the quick motions of moving objects are simply not recorded. The extended motion of otherwise stationary objects, such as trees swaying in the wind, are recorded as ghostly blurs. If the camera moves during exposure, the entire image may blur, or, at the very least, a double image will result. In short, pinhole technology favors a stationary world, but one that appears to be very much in focus.

The absence of adjustable camera controls—lens, shutter, and aperture—means we must operate much as photographers did when the photographic medium was in its infancy. In this way, we will gain insights into the nature of cameras and why old photographs look the way they do.

Types of Pinhole Cameras

A reminder: different types of pinhole cameras will render different perspectives of the world. Rectangular box cameras, in which the film or paper plane is kept flat, will produce normal perspectives without distortion. Cylindrical cameras or those with some curvature of the film plane will exhibit a wide-angle perspective that will amplify distances between camera and object and also create vertical linear distortion. Both types will produce great depth of field.

Color

Color represents a very strong visual message (see chapter 9). Even though you're using black and white photo materials, the world of color can still be yours. As you approach the projects in this book and consider the varying results you will see that color, aside from providing an added level of visual information, can also be used to both eliminate and highlight aspects of an image. Hand-coloring can be applied in a realistic or representational manner. It allows us to depart from reality by reordering the spectral reality that we're accustomed to. Coloring a negative image can remove us even further from perceptual norms. It's great fun to produce copies of the same image and color each one differently. By using opaque color you can paint out parts of an image. Transparent materials allow the underlying photographic image to show through a thin glaze of color. Mixing opaque and transparent color is a great way to experiment with the powers of the spectrum. Coloring an image that can be easily reproduced allows great freedom to experiment, without fear of spoiling the original image.

Pinhole Images Using Color Film and Paper

Color negative film can be used in pinhole photography and processed with the appropriate darkroom restrictions for lighting and chemistry. Pinhole images resulting from color negatives display far less color clarity than images made in cameras with lenses. The results, however, can be very interesting and quite beautiful.

Direct color prints using direct positive paper are also possible. Again, the color quality of the pinhole images is quite different from images produced with a lens; the results have a quality all their own.

Is this self-portrait amusing or unsettling? By placing a wide-angle pinhole camera an inch or so from his nose, Colin McKee creates a radically new self-image! *Photo by Colin McKee*

Your Self-Portrait

What more interesting subject can you begin with than yourself? The first requirement of almost every type of portrait is capturing a good likeness. Since you're using the pinhole camera, you will have to hold perfectly still. The second general requirement for a portrait is that it reveal as much about the subject as possible. There's sure to be at least one revelation to come out of your pinhole self-portrait: Can you hold still?

Technique

The bright light of the outdoors will minimize your exposure time. A really sunny day is best; early morning or late afternoon light will sculpt your features within the framework of its characteristic volume. Place yourself and the camera so that the sun is to one side, at right angles to an imagined line between you and the pinhole. Make sure the camera isn't pointing into the sun.

The most difficult and startling portrait is a bold head shot; you'll fill the paper with your face. Bring the camera really close, especially if the camera has curved sides that will produce a wide-angle perspective.

Unless you brace your head, using arms and hands, or rest your chin or cheek on something solid, you will move, causing a blur. Find a reasonably comfortable position sitting at a bench, leaning against a wall, or lying flat on your stomach. Set your camera down on something solid or use a tripod.

When your position is fixed, carefully uncover the pinhole so as not to jar the camera. Expose for about 20 to 30 seconds. Moving your body as little as possible, sneak up on the camera with your hand and carefully cover the pinhole. Return to the darkroom, uncover the pinhole, and process the image.

Photographing with the camera so close will result in some distortion, particularly with a curved camera. The distortions are usually quite humorous—even so, the initial shock of recognition can be a little uncomfortable; remember, it's only a picture.

After the first image, it may be necessary to adjust exposure time, camera distance, and your position relative to the sun. If some really fine adjustments are necessary, use some chalk to mark the position of camera and body. Make sure you are counting the seconds during exposure. When the exposure is just right, record the results on your camera.

The play of light upon the face will ultimately determine the most effective portrait. Creating the variations requires patience and physical work, but surely the subject is worth the effort. Experiment with frontal and three-quarter views. Try a profile. Good contrast between light and dark is very helpful. If your complexion is light, a dark background will be helpful. If your complexion is dark, provide yourself with a light background. Make sure you remain in the light as you pose yourself and manipulate the camera.

If shadows prove too harsh, try adding some reflected light. Place some white cardboard below or across from the shadow side of your face. The cardboard forms a reflector that will fill in the shadow area, adding detail to the exposed image.

Overcast days require longer exposure time (and the challenge of holding still longer), but the quality of light is less harsh. Shadows melt away, offering a very mellow mood.

Once you've come away with an effective head shot, it's time to try a self-portrait that offers more. Hats, patterned clothing, and props offer endless possibilities for creating a portrait that represents a real personality. Photograph yourself with objects that you associate with the things you like to do, such as a basketball, a book, or a musical instrument.

Historical Byte

In the early years of photography, film of weaker sensitivity, cumbersome equipment, and dangerous chemicals made for an arduous process. Exposure times were long and it wasn't possible to freeze motion. Portrait sessions required the subject to sit very still, often requiring the use of neck braces and other mechanical paraphernalia to limit the movement of the sitter. Even smiling for a portrait was risky; holding a smile isn't easy when exposure time is extended. Rather than risk a failing smile that could easily end in a blurred image, sitting for a portrait required a steady gaze and a neutral facial expression that required no muscle tension. The result was usually an image that seemed void of all emotion. One gets the impression that people of yesteryear lead dull, expressionless lives.

As time and photographic processes improved, the capturing of moments became a technical reality. Such moments revealed the smiles and laughter that usually went unrecorded in earlier days.

Tricks with Scale

Your pinhole camera provides almost unlimited depth of field, so you can play wonderful tricks with the relative scale of objects. You can make objects that are small enough to fit in the palm of a hand appear dramatically larger. A small toy dinosaur can be made to appear larger than its living predecessors. A normal shoe can appear large enough to house the famous old woman who lived in one. A mouse trap can take on the scale of monumental sculpture.

Technique

By placing a small object, like a baseball, inches from the pinhole, and keeping a reasonable distance from something large, like a building or tree, you can create the illusion that

Model makers, take note! Playing tricks with scale is easy with a pinhole camera. This tyrannosaur appears to be emerging from the mists of an upscale swamp ready to throw its weight around the neighborhood. Actually, this plastic T-rex is only 8 inches tall and a few inches from the wide-angle camera; the high rise half a block away is real. *Photo by Evan Kono*

the small object is infinitely larger—larger even than the actual building or tree. Tricks with scale have a dramatic effect based on immediate comparison, on comparing the relative size of a house with that of the ball. The dynamic variables are the distance from the small object to the camera, and of small object and camera from the much larger object in the distance. The larger the big object, the greater the distance it must be from the camera. If you use only small objects, or stand too close to the large-scale object, the resulting image will simply appear as an extreme close-up.

The illusion is most dramatic when the small object is something that fits in the palm of a hand. Let the common, everyday nature of objects guide your choice of subject matter. When a scissors, can opener, or soft drink can appear larger than a house, the effect is startling. You can turn reality on end!

Surprisingly, the major challenge of photographing small objects is the job of making sure they are placed close enough to the pinhole of the camera to be seen. Often, it is necessary to raise the small object high enough to be included in the view of the pinhole. The trick is to support the object without allowing the support mechanism to be visible in the picture.

Supporting the object by raising it up on a block of wood or a small mound of earth will usually solve the problem. A really tricky solution can be borrowed from the professionals by using a small lump of clay than can be molded to fit the situation and easily pierced to offer support.

To create special effects, a small pane of glass can be used as an invisible wall on which to attach objects. Loops of tape or double-sided tape can be used to adhere objects to the glass for short periods of time. If the camera is pointing up, the glass can form an invisible bridge on which objects can be suspended above the camera. The camera itself can be suspended above objects, using a pane of glass. Solving these problems is intrinsic to both the science and the art of photography. Bold simplicity in a picture often requires a great deal of creative engineering.

The Model Builder's Camera

The world of miniature objects can merge easily with life-size reality. You can bridge the gap between human and miniature scale by carefully placing a pinhole camera within a large-scale setting that includes your choice of miniature. A miniature car, airplane, or building can assume a large, even monumental, presence.

In my design class, students produce concept models of sculpture pieces intended for specific settings around the school. When the models are finished, they are placed near the intended site and photographed with a pinhole camera. The resulting images are often hand-colored to provide additional clarity. This form of quick conceptual preview is very convincing!

Technique

A small model of your favorite sports car set in front of your actual house or apartment building can quickly lead to an image that suggests a dream come true. An architectural model of a house placed in close proximity to its proposed site can provide some realistic imaging. A miniature sculpture intended as a model for a larger outdoor or indoor work can be set in the midst of its intended location to produce a simulation of the completed project. Structures made with toy building sets can take on monumental size. With the addition of some hand-coloring, all these miniature projects can be given a large-scale life of their own. On a grander scale the process allows you to visually link a miniature concept to a full-scale environment.

Storyteller's Pinhole Camera

The pinhole camera's ability to play tricks with the scale provides us with a unique means to invent, relate, or illustrate stories. Just as cartoonists create comic strips and art directors produce story boards for television, we can use miniature figures in real settings to relate or invent stories.

This project allows us to reclaim some childhood toys. If I went back to my own toy box I could bring out my Lincoln Logs, Fort Apache, and little Davy Crockett. You don't have to go back that far. I often lead my pinhole camera students to the school's kindergarten where we borrow dinosaurs, cows, and horses.

Technique

Using miniature figures of humans, clay figures of animals, creatures, and machines creates action scenarios in almost any genre. Add the comic strip look by drawing dialogue bubbles when you turn negatives into positives. Use negative images as day-for-night scenes.

See What Mice See

Everyone, at one time or another, wonders what it feels like to be small, really small. Movies depict the adventures of fortunate (or unfortunate) humans shrunk accidentally (or on purpose) to sizes ranging from minuscule to microscopic. If you've ever wondered what the world looks like to a mouse, fly, or micro human, now's your chance. And you needn't worry about marauding cats and spiders.

Technique

Just put your pinhole camera where your mind's eye would like to be: in the terrarium, on the book shelf, among the house plants, between the toaster and the food processor, in your camera bag, on the bathroom floor, looking up at the

Here is a big view of a small world captured with the nondistorting Model 57 pinhole camera: a Turkish coffee grinder and parts of an espresso maker sit atop a kitchen counter. The middle ground reveals a juicing machine, carving knives, and a dish drying rack.

kitchen faucet. Wherever you can put your pinhole camera, you can view the world from a tiny creature's point of view.

A small camera with a curved film plane will take the best advantage of pinhole depth of field and the tricks with scale phenomenon. Being in among the small things often means getting into the shadows. This will often require long exposure times, but the results are worth the extra wait.

Building a Still Life

Photographing small, inanimate objects is usually referred to as still life or tabletop photography. In the distant past, still life painting and photography centered on the rendering of objects that usually had symbolic value: a bowl of fruit on a clean tablecloth symbolized a bountiful earth and simple domesticity; a grand table laden with freshly killed game, bread, wine jugs, cheese, and fruit represented wealth and plenty. Modern advertising is similar in that tabletop photography displays products associated with various lifestyles.

Technique

Given the characteristic advantages of the pinhole, still life photography takes on a new excitement. Using daylight or strong photo flood lamps (500 watts), the lighting of a scene can be as carefully controlled as on a stage set. You can, of course, use pinhole techniques to create or simulate stage set designs. Small figures, miniature furniture, small painted flats can all be assembled and lit to create set designs.

Using mirrors, drawings, and photographs, objects attached to glass or clear acetate sheets, and any combination of objects you care to devise, wonderful still life worlds can be created on the top of a table. Color can be added later.

Multiple Exposures with Pinhole Images

Multiple exposure, or double exposure, is the practice of adding layers of image to a single sheet of film or paper. The results usually appear surreal and bizarre. Often, multiple exposures occur unintentionally when the film in regular cameras fails to advance properly; the frames overlap, resulting in combined images that can appear very exciting. Images and scenes are merged in ways that we might never imagine.

Technique

The technique is simple: you expose the film or paper twice; the resulting images will overlap and merge in unexpected ways. Planning multiple exposures with a pinhole camera doesn't eliminate the element of surprise, it just determines that certain desired subjects will be the *source* of surprise.

The image of a car combined with a second image of a masonry wall will likely appear as a car made of bricks. A close-up of your face and a second image of the rough bark of a tree will become a face made of bark. A first image with your arm extended as if hanging on to a friend and a second image of yourself filling the space where the arm was extended will result in a picture of your arm around yourself.

Under most circumstances exposing film or paper to more than two images produces too many layers of light, hence the term *double exposure*. Light-sensitive materials have limits, and more than two images usually stretches those limits beyond a useful range. Too many layers of imagery become indistinguishable, and light-sensitive material becomes over-exposed, too dense to transmit light for producing positive images.

The most common error in planning a double exposure is overcompensating for the second exposure. Make the expo-sures for the double image as though you were making sepa-rate images: a bright image will be exposed for less time than an image in the shadows. If when viewing the results you decide that one of the two images should dominate, make the exposures again—this time compensating for one image to show through more than the other. More than any other technique, multiple exposure requires trial and error.

It's a good idea to avoid bright sky areas in double expo-sure images. The sky is so bright it will usually eliminate any other image that overlaps it. Give some thought to providing contrast between background and foreground. Placing a light object in front of a darker background and vice versa will help viewers to see objects and forms more easily.

When seeking subjects for multiple exposures, look for stark contrasts: plant and natural forms combined with man-made forms (organic with geometric); light and dark; rough and smooth; transparent and opaque; human and mechani-cal; close and far away.

Pinhole Pictures and Computers

Like any other photograph, pinhole camera images can be used with com-puters. You can use a computer scanning device to save an image on a disk and then manipulate it with graphics programs to create any number of variations. The results can be included in computer program sequences that add text, color, and sound. The results can also be transferred to video or printed.

Painting and Drawing with Pinhole Images

For anyone with a strong interest in drawing, painting, or illustration, the pinhole image can provide great source material for creating and building images. Using pinhole images to draw from, or placing the image in an opaque projector and enlarging it over and over again to fit bigger surfaces are only two of many ways to capitalize on pinhole technology.

Enlarging Small Pinhole Images

Unless you build a very large pinhole camera, pictures will remain relatively small. Small pictures, when mounted and framed, require the viewer to get close for viewing. The intimate quality of small images is a very attractive aspect of the miniature world.

If you want large pinhole pictures, you have two choices: make a large camera and use large paper, trays, and lots of chemicals, or have your favorite pinhole images copied and enlarged.

If you use film to take pinhole pictures, you can simply use the negatives with an enlarger that will accommodate the film format. Projection printing with an enlarger will allow you to make prints as large as you like.

Pinhole pictures made with paper negatives cannot be printed by projection unless a film negative is made. The film negative of a positive pinhole print can be made with any black and white negative film. A slow speed, low ASA-type panchromatic film will produce fine grain images. You can also use film specially made for copy work, extremely low ASA, and no grain.

Pinhole pictures can be copied by using a 35mm camera and a normal distance lens of 50mm. With a normal lens, however, you can only get within 2 or 3 feet of the image. The copied image would represent but a small portion of the total negative, and a copy print would lack the necessary detail and sharpness.

Inexpensive, supplementary close-up lens sets (shallow dish lenses) allow extremely closeup magnification, with image ratios up to 1:1. This means that an object, such as a dime, can appear actual size on the resulting negative. A 5 × 7–inch pinhole image can all but fill the frame of a 35mm copy negative. The resulting enlargement will provide sharp, grain-free detail when made with copy film.

A macro lens for a 35mm format camera offers the best solution for copying small images and photographing small objects. If you have access to a macro lens and a tripod or copy stand, you can easily produce suitable copy negatives for enlarging pinhole images.

Slides or transparencies (chromes) can also be made using the lenses that are suited for close-up photography. You can put together very intriguing slide presentations from pinhole camera images.

Any full service photo finishing establishment or photostat house can also provide enlarged prints to your specifications. When printed on paper with a dull finish, large prints can be easily hand-colored with any of the available materials (see chapter 9), including airbrushing. Large images are easier to see from a distance and make a greater impact, depending on the subject and contrast of the image.

Historical Bytes

Look at some photographs taken early in the history of photography; they will reveal many similarities to your pinhole images. Light-sensitive materials used early on were slow to react to light. Even with the use of adjustable lenses and apertures, the first photographers recorded a stationary world. Pinhole cameras make use of paper and film that is much more sensitive to light that early materials, but your reliance on a simple, tiny pinhole allows you to share a similar disadvantage with the pioneers of photography: the world of action escapes you; the slightest motion takes the form of ghost-like swirls and blurs. A well-known portrait of Abraham Lincoln reveals the iron neck brace used to steady a subject for a blur-free image; the great president does not look happy.

The wooden cameras and tripods of the early days were heavy and not terribly adjustable. Light-sensitive plates were cumbersome. The chemicals were dangerous. The images were harsh, with undue contrast resulting from light-sensitive emulsion that reacted primarily to blue light. Red, orange, and yellow, the colors that produce a familiar range of gray tones, were not well represented. By today's standards, the art and practice of photography was a crude and labor-intensive activity. Fortunately for photographers, everyone wanted to be photographed.

Additional Reading

Copying and Duplicating In Black-and-White and Color, W. Arthur Young, coauthor and editor; Thomas A. Benson, coauthor and assistant editor; George T. Eaton, coauthor. Eastman Kodak Co., 1984.

A picture made with the Pinhole 360 presents a continuous all-around image. This city skyline scene captures the combined effects of the camera's four apertures. The four images overlap and produce disjointed segments. The lightest section indicates the position of the sun. The overlapping creates merging shapes reminiscent of early Cubist and Fauve paintings.

6 | A Quick Course in Camera Work

Knowing how your camera works will give you more confidence in your photography.

Controlling Light with Cameras

The how-to revolution seems to have started with photography. There is a great wealth of photographic information on book and camera store shelves. Publications, videos, seminars, and workshops are readily available to instruct us in the use of every type of photographic material, tool, process, and specialty. I don't want to duplicate what has already been done so thoroughly by others. This quick course in camera work is intended to provide the novice with an objective place to begin taking pictures with a variety of manufactured cameras.

The Bare Essentials

Light is the primary ingredient. We must deal with time, space, and motion. Building and using a pinhole camera teaches us what is essential in the making of photographs: a light-tight container, blackened on the inside, with a tiny hole that introduces light. The pinhole aperture allows reflected light into the camera, to be focused on the film. Trial and error teaches us that exposure time varies with available light levels. Counting or keeping an eye on the second-hand of your watch and moving your finger over the pinhole dealt with time differences. Everything is designed to control the light available to you, and experimenting sharpens your judgment.

The Complete Camera

A complete camera offers a good deal more than a pinhole when it comes to measuring and controlling light. Choosing a camera is no longer a simple task. Contemporary photography offers a dazzling array of camera choices. The range of optical, mechanical, and electronic camera technology is broad and often confusing. Smart, computer-educated, battery-driven, automatic cameras are present in great numbers. The older, simple, basic mechanical camera is hard to find. Soon the manually operated camera may become just another collector's item.

It's comforting to know that despite the computerized nature of camera technology, the essential controls remain the same. Every camera, regardless of the advanced technology designed into it, has three primary controls—the same controls that have been present for over one hundred years—and mastering them remains essential to the art and craft of photography.

The Primary Controls

The primary camera mechanisms that allow us to control light and deal with time, space, and motion are the aperture, the lens, and the shutter. Most newer cameras also include an exposure meter equipped with an adjustable film-sensitivity setting (ASA and DIN).

THE APERTURE

Using a pinhole camera is a great lesson in the value of a simple aperture. The modern aperture controls the volume of light that enters the camera and is also adjustable. The tiny aperture of a pinhole camera provides great depth of field. Modern apertures provide the same service, but not in such generous measure. The apertures for manufactured cameras are built into the lens, or, as in the case of some apertures, allow lens elements to be attached. In all cases, lens and aperture operate together.

Aperture openings are referred to as f-stops. F stands for the word factor, a mathematical term. A series of f-stops, on any lens, is arranged so that the smallest number represents the largest aperture opening. For example, f/2 would be the largest aperture opening in a series that ended with f/16, the smallest opening. The entire series of numbered openings would include f/2, f/4, f/5.6, f/8, f/11, and f/16. On most cameras, aperture numbers are engraved on the aperture control, a movable ring that circles the lens barrel. The ring is attached to an adjustable diaphragm made of thin metal leaves. As the ring is adjusted, the metal leaves create an opening shaped like a hexagon.

The Lens

Optics, the science of making and using lenses, remains the essence of photographic technology. The lens of a camera has the function of gathering light and focusing it evenly on the film plane. The lens also allows us to focus on different points in space, which are referred to as points of critical focus. The points are actually planes, like sheets of glass. Any object on the same plane of critical focus will be in seen in sharp focus.

If this were not enough, different lenses are often available for the same camera, providing a choice of perspective. Normal lenses offer a perspective of the world as seen by our eyes. Wide-angle lenses broaden our perspective and make the world appear more spacious from edge to edge and from foreground to background. Telephoto lenses bring distant objects closer and make the world look somewhat flat. Macro lenses magnify the world.

Producing lenses that create different perspectives requires that lens construction vary. Most good camera lenses are made up of several lens elements held in a tube. The distance between these lens elements changes as we change focus. A wide-angle lens tube must be of short construction to allow wider angle of view. A telephoto lens tube must be long, to allow for the increased spacing of lens elements that will magnify distant images. Each lens type must be capable of focusing at infinity: the farthest reaches of our vision. At infinity we see the distant horizon, clouds in the sky, and the moon. The distance between the rear element of any lens we are using and the film plane of the camera, when the lens is focused at infinity, is called the focal length of the lens. The infinity setting is marked on the lens where the focusing extension stops. The symbol for infinity looks like a horizontal figure eight. The focal length of the lens is marked on the front of the lens, along with the widest aperture the lens is capable of opening to (50mm, f/2).

Lenses for many types of cameras also have markings that tell us how far we are from the point of critical focus, as well as the distances at which depth of field will begin and end. Many of the newest lenses focus automatically by means of an infrared beam.

The simplest lenses on cameras of limited technology are preset, along with aperture openings, to provide reasonably sharp images with adequate depth of field under bright daylight or short-range electronic flash.

Aperture and Lens Control Depth of Field

The aperture and the lens have a special relationship. The focusing power of the lens, combined with the ability of the aperture to vary the volume of light passing through the lens, work in tandem to determine depth of field.

Depth of field, you'll recall, refers to that part of an image that is in sharp focus. Extreme depth of field (also called depth of focus) occurs when an entire image, from foreground to background, is in sharp focus. As with the pinhole camera, extreme depth of field occurs when virtually all the light that enters the lens, through the aperture, is focused on the film plane. The complete camera, unlike its pinhole cousin, provides sharp images from center to edge along with adjustable depth of field.

As the aperture in the lens is opened wider, more light enters. As the volume of light increases, the lens becomes less efficient at focusing all the light on the film plane; more of the light bounces around, creating images that appear less focused, and the depth of field narrows. As the aperture continues to open, the depth of field decreases until only the narrow plane of critical focus is sharp and clear.

There are three variables that determine depth of field: the aperture opening (the smaller the aperture, the greater the depth of field), the lens (the shorter the focal length of the lens, the greater the depth of field at any common f-stop; wide-angle lenses are short, telephoto lenses are long), and subject-camera distance (the farther from the subject you are, the greater the depth of field you can have).

THE SHUTTER

The camera shutter allows us to deal with time in a number of ways. The shutter determines the length of time that light is allowed to strike the film. Most photographs are made with the intention of stopping motion. To do so, the length of time the shutter remains open must be extremely short. Some pictures are taken to record motion, such as the blur of a fast car. These images require shutter speeds that are fast, but not too fast. Where light levels are low and extreme depth of field is required, a shutter may be opened for long periods of time, with the camera mounted on a tripod.

Shutter speeds can vary from several thousandths of a second to a full second, or more. Many shutters have a setting labeled B; this setting allows us to keep the shutter open indefinitely. The usual range of shutter speeds on adjustable and automatic cameras start with the B setting. Next comes the number 1 which stands for 1 full second. This is followed by 2, or 1/2 of a second. All the numbers that follow represent fractions of 1 second. Four equals 1/4 of a second. Five hundred equals 1/500 of a second. The usual sequence of shutter speeds is as follows: B, 1, 2, 4, 8, 15, 30, 60, 125, 250, 500, 1000. The shutter speed control is usually located either on the top of the camera body or on a ring surrounding the lens.

There are two kinds of shutters: the leaf shutter and the focal plane shutter. The leaf shutter is part of the lens structure. It is so named because its metal sections resemble leaves. It opens and closes in the usual timed fashion and also forms the openings of the aperture. In this case, shutter and aperture are one and the same device, with separate controls that determine shutter speed and aperture size.

The focal plane shutter is part of the camera body, and as the name implies, it is located between the path of the film and the lens. The focal plane shutter is like a window shade with an open slot that passes the film at different speeds. Cameras, such as 35mm single lens reflex (SLR) models, have focal plane shutters in the body of the camera. This allows for the ease and thrift of using many interchangeable lenses on a single camera body equipped with one shutter.

SHUTTER, APERTURE, AND GEOMETRIC PROGRESSION

The mechanics of balancing shutter speeds and aperture openings is made easier by the manner in which shutter and aperture work. Both controls measure out their respective elements using a mathematical system known as geometric progression. Geometric progression is a system of incremental change whereby quantities either double in size or are reduced by half.

In practical terms this means that if we increase the speed of the shutter from 1 second to 1/2 of a second, the speed of the shutter is doubled. And if we change the aperture from f/16 to f/11, we are allowing the volume of light to double. It also means that when we decrease the time or volume of light by a single move of the control, we are reducing it by half. Once this important relationship is understood, the mechanics of choosing between aperture opening and shutter speed will also aid us in maintaining the proper exposure.

THE EXPOSURE METER

One of the newest devices built into modern cameras is the exposure meter, also called a light meter. Exposure meters are also available as separate devices. They operate using battery powered memory chips. Part of the meter is a calibration control that allows the photographer to adjust the exposure meter to the sensitivity of the film being used (ASA).

The exposure meter measures light levels. It is the bridge that connects the primary controls of the camera to the particular lighting conditions we face when taking pictures. When the exposure meter measures the light that illuminates a scene the silicone memory chip presents us with a set of paired shutter and aperture combinations. Using any of the paired combinations will result in properly exposed film.

Many types of cameras in use today have no built-in exposure meters. These cameras require no mechanical or electronic connection to an exposure meter to allow the primary controls to function. Instead, photographers use hand-held exposure meters to measure light levels. The effect is the same: a range of usable shutter and aperture settings is aligned for our selection.

The Sensitivity of Film

Film and other light-sensitive materials are tested for their relative sensitivity to light. The American Standards Association (ASA), an independent testing laboratory, conducts the testing. The results of the tests are expressed in terms of direct arithmetic: film rated at 100 ASA is twice as sensitive to light as film rated at 50 ASA. ASA 400 film is four times more sensitive to light than 100 ASA film. The abbreviation ISO (International Standardization Organization) is also used in place of ASA. The European equivalent to ASA numbers is the DIN standard (Deutsche Industrie Norm). These numbers appear on film packaging and instruction sheets. They will also be found on camera and exposure meter controls.

Failure to set the ASA properly may result in film that is poorly exposed. Many newer cameras are equipped with a device called a DX code, which is imprinted on the film and automatically reads and sets the ASA rating.

SHUTTER, APERTURE, AND EXPOSURE METER TOGETHER

There must always be an aperture opening and there must always be a shutter speed. Shutter and aperture are an inseparable team. Choosing the proper combination of shutter speed and aperture opening is the constant choice that photographers make.

Again, by calibrating the exposure meter to the sensitivity range of the film we are using, we will be presented with a series of recommended shutter and aperture combinations that will allow our film to be properly exposed. However—and this is a warning as well as a qualification—a properly exposed image isn't always the picture we expect. The degree to which motion is stopped or allowed to blur, the extent of the depth of field, and the quality of exposure in the bright and shadow areas, are all tied to the same set of choices. To say it another way: any combination of shutter and aperture arrived at by correct use of the exposure meter will result in proper exposure. Whereas, the best image will likely be the result of a careful choice of just one or two of the possible combinations, the combination that effectively deals with motion or provides the proper depth of field.

We photographers choose a shutter-aperture combination according to our primary intentions. For example, if we intend to stop motion we must first choose a fast shutter speed and then accept the appropriate aperture setting indicated by the exposure meter. On the other hand, if we desire maximum depth of field we choose the smallest aperture opening possible, as indicated by our exposure meter. We follow up our choice by accepting the indicated shutter speed that has been paired up with our choice of aperture on the exposure meter.

The absence of light or too much light often requires that we compromise when choosing shutter-aperture combinations. For example, in bright circumstances stopping action and producing extreme depth of field is easy. But when the light level is low, the combination of stopping action and producing depth of field can be a problem. If action must be frozen under dim light, the shutter speed must remain fast. The exposure meter will indicate that the aperture must be opened wider to let in more light, insuring proper exposure. By opening up the aperture, however, we sacrifice depth of field. If the most important goal is to stop action, we must compromise and limit the depth of field.

If we had absolute control over the level of available light there would be no need to compromise. We would simply increase the amount of light until all our requirements were met. Unless we are taking pictures in a studio equipped with unlimited lighting possibilities, the idea of unlimited control over light is unrealistic.

The Requirements of Light and Image

It is clear that choosing a shutter-aperture combination starts with measuring the light level to see what choices are available to us. Often the choice is one of stopping action or controlling depth of field, which is even more complicated when we consider that film is not nearly as sensitive as our own visual powers. Unlike the eye, film is not capable of recording information from both the brightest and darkest parts of normal sunlit scenes. Only when the difference between the lightest and the darkest part of a scene is minimal (low contrast) can film record everything. The relative insensitivity of film means that we have yet another choice to make if lighting contrast is dramatic, as in a sunlit scene at midday. We must choose between the bright half or the dark half of the scene before us. One or the other will be exposed too much or too little.

FILM SIZE AND IMAGE QUALITY

A variety of film formats (sizes) is available to the photographer. The larger the format of the negative, the greater the detail and enlarging power of the film. Large film formats require large cameras and enlargers.

Solving Problems with Cameras

Your choice of camera should be determined by what you wish to accomplish. Your photographic desires may be short-term: to simply take some vacation pictures, or document a birthday party and consign your output to a photo album. Or you may have volunteered to be photo editor of your school yearbook with some serious deadlines to meet and a wide variety of situations to photograph. It may be that you wish to know everything there is to know about the medium. Whatever your inclination or predicament, there's a camera out there for you—many cameras, if you like, depending on the task at hand.

Since we use cameras to increase our ability to see and record images, the special challenge is not to encumber ourselves with tools and technologies that may get in the way of clear vision. Another way to acknowledge the challenge is to make use of the fewest number of hand-held tools to do the greatest amount of visual work. In this way, we can sharpen our vision and gain a solid grounding in the capabilities of the most common and available photographic tools. The first order of business is to see as clearly as possible what's out there in front of us.

Camera Types and Uses

THE DISPOSABLE CAMERA

In 1888 George Eastman introduced the Kodak Camera. He urged everyone to be a photographer by offering a camera loaded with film: "You push the button, we do the rest." When all the pictures were taken the camera was returned to Kodak. Soon, finished pictures came back along with new film in the same camera.

The popular photographic industry has almost come full circle with the recent introduction of the disposable camera. Today we can buy a cardboard and plastic camera containing film. When the pictures are taken the camera is turned in and the photos are processed. We get color negatives and finished pictures. If we want more we buy a new camera loaded with new film. No expensive investment, batteries, repairs, or insurance worries, just color prints and color negatives. The color negatives can produce color as well as black and white prints.

Disposable cameras come in the form of outdoor models with both normal and panoramic formats as well as water resistant/underwater functions. An indoor/outdoor model comes with a built-in flash unit. All film is color negative material. These are prefocused, fixed aperture/shutter speed cameras with medium speed film. They provide some stop-action and reasonable depth of field under daylight and close-in flash situations. Don't look for big enlargements unless you want fuzzy, impressionistic images (and you might just want that from a disposable camera!).

Disposables are a lot of fun. We can take them places and do things with them that we wouldn't want to risk with an expensive camera. It's a challenging camera because of the limitations, but it will invite your powers of invention.

POINT AND SHOOT CAMERAS

Point and shoot cameras are by far the most popular cameras currently in use. Most have built-in flash units, adjustable DX codes (ASA selection), auto advance mechanisms, a limited choice of focusing options, and limited choice of aperture. They are reasonably sturdy and some have telephoto capability. Most people seem to have one. The newest versions take 35mm film, black and white or color. Most people shoot color film.

Point and shoot cameras are fun, somewhat adjustable, and reliable, so long as you learn the limitations. Many professionals carry one as an emergency, do anything, throwaway camera! If it's lost, broken, or confiscated, so what? The images are fairly sharp, but do not take well to big enlargement.

Most amateur photographers own some form of point-and-shoot camera. It might surprise you to know that many professionals also own one.

A few of these cameras, with their fine lenses, light meters, and excellent material construction are very expensive! They allow for sharper images, bigger enlargements, and more control over lighting situations.

Because of compact design requirements, the lenses in many of these cameras have short focal length, moderate wide-angle prescriptions. Wide-angle lenses offer advantages where depth of field and panoramic perspective are required.

INSTANT CAMERAS AND FILM

Instant film cameras are famous for no-wait photography. The new amateur cameras have built-in flash and limited aperture and focusing adjustments. Film processing is done inside the camera when processing chemicals are squeezed over newly exposed film with transport rollers. Recent improvements have increased the sharpness of the image.

Instant film can be manipulated to some degree. The film's emulsion, protected by a clear, transparent material, can be pushed and pressured, displacing the image created by the lens. The results vary depending on pressure and type of tool used; the effect appears to be a combination of photographic image and drawing.

Larger formats of instant film are available in color and black and white. These formats are loaded into film backs, which fit onto various types of view cameras (see The View Camera, later in this chapter). Special film backs are also available for medium format cameras.

Professional photographers often use instant film, color and black and white, for making test shots. Lighting effects, composition, perspective, and depth of field are tested with instant film. The final exposures are then made with film that produces transparencies or film negatives. Some new forms of instant film are used to make final images, including color slides. Instant film is widely used for many scientific and research functions.

ADJUSTABLE RANGE FINDER CAMERAS

A range finder is an optical device that determines distances. In a range finder-style camera the device is coupled with the camera lens to allow the photographer to focus the lens accurately. Range finder viewing is similar to looking out a window with lines drawn around the edge to mark the picture area. A double image mechanism appears in the center of the viewer. As the camera operator focuses on an object centered in the viewer, the double image merges into a single image when sharp focus is achieved. The range finder allows continuous viewing of the subject, as well as a view that is usually wider than the actual picture area; this means the photographer can see objects that are about to enter the picture area. The advantage of the range finder is that it in no way limits our view of the scene.

This is especially helpful when dark, colored filters are being used over the lens; they are not a problem for someone using the range finder.

SINGLE LENS REFLEX CAMERAS

Reflex cameras allow the subject to be viewed through the lens that will take the picture. This is accomplished by means of a mirrored device similar to a periscope. The camera operator looks through a viewer containing angled mirrors. The lower mirror is hinged between the shutter and the lens opening. We get what we see, in terms of picture area and point of critical focus. Depth of field may change; when we view and focus with the reflex mechanism, we do so with the aperture wide open. This allows for bright viewing and the ability to see the point of critical focus change as we focus the lens. When we're ready to make an exposure, the lower mirror flexes out of the shutter's way, the aperture setting we've chosen will be set automatically, and the shutter will open and close. With exposure completed, the lower reflex mirror will flex back into viewing position, and the lens aperture will open wide again. While all this synchronized movement is taking place the viewing mechanism is closed. Many single lens reflex cameras offer a depth-of-field preview function. When our aperture is set to something other than the largest opening, the preview device allows the aperture to change to the setting we've chosen. We can then see what the depth of field will look like in the final picture. However, if we've chosen a small aperture, the light entering the lens will be faint and seeing clearly will be difficult. Most photographers rely on the depth of field scale engraved on almost all SLR lenses.

The SLR has many advantages, such as portability, easy viewing and focusing, interchangeable lenses, and many models and makers to choose from. The 35mm SLR is the most popular advanced camera type presently in use.

A few SLR's are designed to be used with medium format films. They often have interchangeable film backs and use interchangeable lenses that also contain leaf shutters.

THE TWIN LENS REFLEX CAMERA

As the name implies, the twin lens reflex camera makes use of two lenses to view and take pictures. The lenses are arranged one over the other. The top lens is the viewing lens, connected to a reflex mirror and the viewing glass, which is located on the top surface of the camera. The bottom lens is the taking lens; it contains the leaf shutter and aperture.

Twin lens reflex cameras are designed to use medium-size film formats (2¼ × 2¼ inches, 2¼ × 2¾ inches, etc.). Some are available with interchangeable lenses.

The advantage of the twin lens reflex camera is that the image is viewed on ground glass and approximates the final photograph in terms of its flat, graphic quality. Also, the viewing mechanism is never closed while film is being exposed.

THE VIEW CAMERA

The view camera is the oldest of camera types and is still in use today. Though the design is simple, it's capable of relatively complex adjustments. These adjustments allow for the control of perspective and distortion that we can only accept when using other types of cameras.

The view camera is essentially two parallel frames connected by a flexible bellows. The frames are mounted on a single rail, or flat bed. The front frame holds a lens, with a shutter and aperture. The rear frame contains a ground glass and allows for the glass to be displaced by a holder containing film.

The front and back frames of the camera move independently. They can be raised, lowered, swung, and tilted. By manipulating the front lens plane and the rear film plane various forms of distortion can be eliminated, or exaggerated.

The most common form of distortion is seen in parallel lines that converge, as in photos of tall buildings: the vertical lines converge when shot with a normal camera. When using a view camera, the front and back of the camera can be arranged in such a way that the vertical lines in the scene remain vertical.

View cameras are used with large format film (4×5, 8×10, and 11×14 inches and larger). The large negative offers the greatest possible detail and print quality. The view camera is difficult to master and not suitable for agile picture-taking. It is used most often in commercial product photography, architectural, landscape, and portrait work.

The press camera and field camera are variations of the view camera. The press and field cameras are designed for the rigors of outdoor location work and even hand-held journalistic photography. Before the 35mm format became so widely used and improved, the 4×5–inch press camera was the workhorse of newspaper photographers everywhere. It's the clunky camera with the big flash we see in all the old movies, one of the most flexible camera types ever made and one that continues to offer wonderful image quality.

Large format negatives can be contact printed or enlarged to create huge, finely detailed prints with more tonal content per square inch than can be found in small format enlargements.

All types of view cameras can be used for pinhole photography. Just remove the lens and replace it with a pinhole aperture. Regular view camera film holders, as well as instant film backs and film, can be used in the pinhole process.

The Well-Equipped Photographer

The well-equipped photographer's needs go beyond having a camera. Other tools contribute a great deal to the photographic cause.

THE EXPOSURE METER

Our link to the controls of any camera and the prevailing light is the exposure meter. It is possible to do without such a device, since the range of outdoor light is not unlimited. One can commit to memory shutter and aperture combinations that have rendered good results in the past under bright sunlight, cloudy skies, and hazy conditions. Many professionals and amateurs do it all the time.

Difficult lighting situations involving low light levels, electronic flash, incandescent light, and combinations of these and other types of lighting usually require a measured response. Since light is the photographer's medium, it becomes important to be able to measure light and respond to it, depending upon the problem you face and the results you wish to obtain.

There are exposure meters that measure both continuous light and electronic flash. Spot meters measure limited areas of light. Color meters measure the color temperature of various light sources.

ELECTRONIC FLASH

So many newer cameras have a built-in electronic flash that most photographers already possess this handy light source. Flash units are the most portable source of artificial light. They are powered by a wide variety of batteries as well as power packs that plug into household current. The light source, an electrically charged tube filled with xenon gas, is designed to emit bursts that simulate daylight. Flash units range in size from an ice cube to a coffee pot. Some are designed to attach to cameras, others are placed on light stands and used with reflectors. A few are called dedicated units and are used with specific camera models. Some form of flash unit should be part of every photographer's equipment list.

THE 18 PERCENT GRAY CARD

An 18 percent gray card is the standard middle gray tone and texture to which light meters are calibrated. The opposite side of the card is white and the difference between the two sides, as measured in f-stops, is 5 whole stops. The entire value scale, created by 1-stop differences in exposure, extends from black to white in ten exposures.

When any exposure meter measures the light reflecting off an object and the reading is used to calculate a normal exposure, with normal processing and printing, the object should be rendered the same middle gray as the card. The gray card represents the key photographic standard for exposing and processing light-sensitive materials and testing photographic equipment.

TRIPOD

Freedom of movement is what most camera users have in mind. Perhaps the most enduring symbol of photography is the photojournalist, following the action everywhere. Most professionals, however, rely on the tripod for the sharpest possible photographic images, especially when big enlargements are desired. It's good practice to use the tripod whenever the situation permits. Photographing with large cameras and long exposures are the most obvious situations requiring the use of a tripod. Pinhole cameras and inexpensive cameras that have fixed shutter speeds can produce sharper images if attached to tripods, even if you simply tape the camera in place.

CABLE RELEASE

The cable release, or pneumatic tube with squeeze bulb, are essential for tripping the shutter of a camera when it's mounted on a tripod. The shutter is tripped without any undue motion that will affect the exposure. Though the same result can be had if a camera is equipped with a timer, the cable release provides more control when exact timing is required. A cable release can also be used even when a camera is not on a tripod. There are times when a tripod is not handy and it's useful to set a camera down on a steady surface. If the camera has no timer, or exposure must be coordinated with split-second timing, a cable release is essential.

LENS SHADE

A lens shade is a light-blocking device attached to the end of a lens. The shade prevents nonessential light from entering the lens and creating contrast-reducing flare. Flare is excess light that bounces around inside a lens, reducing the sharpness and clarity of images.

LENS FILTERS

There are many different types of filters for lenses. Colored filters for black and white films change the value relationships depending upon the color of the filter. A particular colored filter will transmit its own color easily and hold back its complementary color (see chapter 9). The color passing freely will appear denser on a black and white negative and a lighter value on a print. The complementary color that is held back will appear less dense on a negative and darker in a print.

Panchromatic film, though it is sensitive to all colors in the visible spectrum, is more sensitive to blue light and less sensitive to red and red-orange. To compensate for the film's extra sensitivity to blue light, I recommend a light yellow filter in daylight situations.

Filters used with color slide films are designed to provide warmer or cooler renditions of the color spectrum.

Some filters are meant to protect the lens from possible damage. There are a wide variety of useful filters designed to increase our control over color and value.

INEXPENSIVE FILM HANDLING

The cost of film is a major expense. There are ways, however, to greatly reduce the cost. If you plan to take a lot of pictures you should consider purchasing film in bulk. Most types of color and black and white 35mm film can be purchased in rolls of 50, 100, and 200 feet. Film can be stored for long periods by refrigeration or freezing. If you purchase bulk film, you can use a portion of the total amount, carefully place the remainder back in its protective tin can, and retape the opening. Then place the can in double plastic bags, sealing each bag with tape or a twist tie. Keep the film cool until you need more, then just remove the sealed plastic bag from the refrigerator or freezer and allow the entire package to warm up to room temperature. Be sure not to remove the film from the sealed plastic bag until the warming or thawing is complete, otherwise moisture will condense on the film itself and ruin the emulsion.

Bulk Film Loading

To make use of bulk film you need a bulk film loader. This device allows film to be stored and loaded into cassettes similar to those used in prepackaged film. You can purchase reusable film cassettes and, using the bulk film loader, provide yourself with cassettes of film with up to 36 exposures.

Bulk film is transferred to the bulk film loader in total darkness; then individual cassettes can be filled in normal room lighting or outdoors in subdued light. The bulk film loader should be kept in a dry, cool place when film is being stored inside for short periods of time. Loading film into cassettes requires only a scissors and masking tape. For details on storing film, refer to the film manufacturer's instructions.

Camera Practice

Using any camera, particularly one with full controls, requires practice. The first and most important aspect of practice is looking through the viewing mechanism. You must train yourself to see with and through your camera.

A pinhole camera doesn't allow you this opportunity. A disposable camera will render a reasonably accurate version of what you see through its sights. Range finder cameras require special practice seeing the split image, and reflex cameras offer the challenge of total change of focus. View cameras require careful looking and many types of adjustment. All cameras require practice.

Composing/Framing Pictures

When we view the world through a frame, something special happens: we start selecting images in a new and more precise way. Our own selection process, with its combination of peripheral vision and pinpoint focusing, represents two extreme modes of seeing. The frame of a camera offers something quite different in terms of selection. "Framing," in photographic terms, is the act of selecting a precise and well-defined field of vision. The alternate term is "composing." Both terms refer to the act of deciding exactly how your picture will look and what will appear in your field of vision.

The shape of the field, in practical terms, is rectangular or square, and it falls far short of your peripheral vision. In the end, the framed image will, if you choose, provide a picture containing great depth of field, another element foreign to your natural eye. It's no wonder that looking through the camera requires practice.

Framing, or composing, is a matter of visual common sense; there are no hard-and-fast rules. There are also many approaches to composing pictures that rely on dividing the frame into general areas such as foreground, middle ground, and background.

Occasional photographers often develop the habit of always placing important subjects in the center of the image area. In doing so they also, quite literally, lose sight of what else appears in the picture. The subject of a picture can just as easily be placed at one side, with other elements in the picture leading the viewer's eye to the subject.

Getting close to what interests you and eliminating superfluous material is one of the most valuable habits you can cultivate for framing. The occasional photographer will often isolate the subject in the center of vast spaces; we end up wondering what the real subject of the picture is.

One major goal in framing is to isolate compositional elements that keep the viewer's eye within the image. Strong directional lines often lead the eye out of a picture. Strive to use visual elements that form a picture in such a way as to keep the eye circulating throughout the picture area, revisiting the forms, shapes, and textures contained in the photo.

The ultimate objective of spending time looking through the camera is to accustom yourself to taking in the whole frame: center, corners, edges—the entire viewing area. Learn to observe the contents of the entire frame, even when you are primarily interested in only a small portion of what is contained therein. You will get everything in the frame, whether you notice it or not. The objective is to notice everything! We say of those who learn to see well through the camera—those who come away with what they really wanted—that he or she *has a good eye*.

Bracketing Exposures

When faced with difficult lighting situations, such as extreme contrast, or dramatic atmospheric conditions like fog, the most useful technique for coming away with a good exposure is bracketing. Simply put, bracketing means making three exposures of a scene: one exposure according to the meter, the second exposure 1 stop underexposed, and the third exposure 1 stop overexposed. Or, to say it another way: one over, one normal, one under. It's not always possible or necessary to engage in bracketing, but when there's adequate time and the lighting is dramatic, bracketing provides some exposure insurance!

Additional Reading

The Camera and Its Images by Arthur Goldsmith. A Ridge Press Book, Newsweek Books, 1979.

The Camera Life Library of Photography. Time-Life Books, 1972.

Camera: The New Ansel Adams Photography Series, Book 1 by Ansel Adams. New York Graphic Society Book, Little, Brown and Company, 1985.

The View Camera: Operations and Techniques by Harvey Shaman. Amphoto, 1977.

7 | Processing Film and Making Prints

Creative control is the ultimate reward for processing your own film and prints. These negatives can be examined directly to decide which to enlarge, or they can all be placed into a printing frame to produce a proof sheet.

The Darkroom

The complete photographic process begins in the mind, is decided by the eye, takes shape in the camera, and is brought to full realization in the darkroom. Exposing film is only the beginning. Every step of the process—developing film, making proofs, printing, and presentation—represents an opportunity for creative interpretation.

What happens in the darkroom represents the creative completion, the finale of creative photography. The famous photographer and darkroom technician Ansel Adams likened the act of making an exposure and developing a negative to composing a musical score. He hastened to add that making a print from the negative was much like performing the music one had composed. What musician would write the music and not play it? It's possible to compose music and let others do the performing. Only the composer, however, can play the music with complete authority. And so it is with our own photographs.

It's possible to take pictures and have all of the film, proofs, and prints processed by photo finishing houses. Many photo finishing establishments offer a complete menu of services to photographers, most of whom are professionals too busy taking pictures to process film and make prints.

Granted, you may not have the time or desire to do all of the processing necessary to provide yourself with fine prints. However, learning about the process will enable you to know what is possible. When you ask others to finish your photographs you'll know what to ask for and how to communicate your creative wishes.

Thus far, the darkroom has been a studio and laboratory where your photographic projects have involved taking full advantage of the basic elements of photography. With the addition of several important tools, the studio/lab can become a full-fledged darkroom. A complete facility will allow you to have control over the full range of photographic possibilities.

Film Processing

There are a number of reasons why developing your own film is worthwhile. First, the process is reasonably simple and quick. For a small investment you can provide yourself with the necessary hardware. If you take a lot of pictures you can enjoy financial savings.

Second, though we can achieve good results by using film at suggested ASA ratings and processing film under recommended "normal" conditions, variations in the film developing process allow us to compensate for many limitations imposed by film. For example, on bright, sunny days it is often difficult to gain adequate shadow detail and prevent dense highlights in our black and white images. To gain what will appear as a normal range of contrast, it is common practice to overexpose the film when taking pictures and underdevelop the film when processing the negatives. This provides for detail in the shadows and prevents excessive density in the highlights.

On a gray day, when contrast is low, it is common practice to underexpose when photographing and overdevelop when processing film. This produces negatives and prints with higher overall contrast. These procedures can make the difference between mediocre and excellent results.

Third, many of the highly creative images we admire are, in great part, due to the film processing techniques used to exaggerate certain visual effects. An image can be made to look harsh by overdeveloping or soft by underdeveloping during film processing. When film is processed in such a way as to push it beyond its ability to produce its optimal characteristics, such as sharpness and clarity of texture, images take on a textured look. At times, this is desirable.

Fourth, errors made when shooting pictures can be compensated for in the processing of film. It's not uncommon to forget to set the ASA accurately. If it was set too high and film is underexposed, the film can be "pushed" (developed longer) to bring forth the image. The results will not be the same as if no error had been made, but the images can likely be saved. Accidental overexposure can be dealt with by underdeveloping the film. Again, the results will not be optimal, but usable images can be obtained. The usable results of both errors will appear to lack the proper contrast.

Finally, most film processing results in the production of negatives; it's the negative that gets printed. The negative is our most important product and it deserves much thought and careful handling. "When you want something done right . . ."

Film Processing and Equipment

FILM PROCESSING ESSENTIALS

- processing canister and reels
- processing thermometer
- timer
- four plastic chemical containers
- water bath tub for chemicals
- darkroom or changing bag
- film-drying clips and weights
- negative storage containers

Film can be processed in trays, tanks, or a closed canister. Sheet film, used with view cameras, is usually processed in open trays or tanks; this requires complete darkness in the processing room. Roll film can be processed in canisters, with tops and lids that keep out light, allowing chemicals to be introduced, agitated, and emptied. This allows the processing steps to be carried out in normal light. There is at least one light-tight tank available for processing sheet film in similar fashion.

For roll film, I recommend using a processing tank, with plastic lid and cap. The tank is used with spiraling reels that exploit tension to suspend the film between the spiraling segments. This method allows chemicals to surround the entire surface of the film.

When picture taking is finished, the film is rewound into the cassette and then removed from the camera. Film cassette, canister, reel(s), and scissors are placed in a changing bag, or the lights in the darkroom are extinguished. The cassette is opened and the film transferred, in complete darkness, from the cassette to a reel. The reel is then placed in the canister.

When the lid is firmly in place on the canister, processing is completed under incandescent light or fluorescent light that does not produce afterglow.

The actual processing consists of subjecting the film in the canister to successive baths of developer, stop bath, fixer, water rinse, hypo clearing

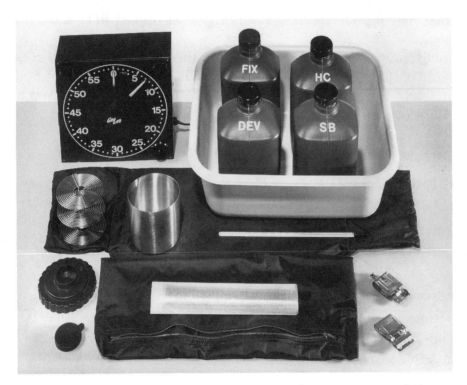

Processing your own film and prints is the ultimate extension of your creative control. The necessary equipment for processing your film includes a timer, chemical and rinsing containers, a stainless steel developing tank with lid and cap, 35mm reels, a processing thermometer, changing bag, hanging clips, and negative storage sleeves.

agent, a final water rinse cycle, and a dip-in wetting agent. While the film is immersed in each successive chemical, it must be vigorously agitated in various ways, to insure that fresh chemical is constantly brought to the light-sensitive emulsion. Finally, the film is hung up to dry in a dust-free area.

The entire active process, from loading reels to hanging the film to dry, requires approximately 40 minutes. Many rolls of film can be processed at one time depending on the capacity of the processing canister and the number of reels in use. Reels must vary in width depending on the format of the film. Some reels are adjustable, accommodating more than one film format.

Black and white negatives, color negatives, and direct positive slide film can all be processed in essentially the same manner. The details of timing and chemistry vary with the type of film being processed.

Developers used to process film are different from paper developers. Stop bath is used in most film processing. The fixer/hypo is generally the same as that used in making prints. Color processes make use of additional chemicals, such as photographic bleach.

Controlling the Process

All film processing requires precise control over the temperature of processing chemistry, including rinse water. In almost every instance, all chemicals used in a single developing cycle must be brought to the same temperature. The temperature of chemicals is usually controlled by placing individual containers of chemicals in a single bath. Running water is brought to the proper temperature and that temperature is maintained. Processing begins when all the chemicals are brought to the proper temperature.

Precise developing times vary depending on several factors, the most important being the dilution and temperature of the developer solution. The stop bath, fixer, and hypo clearing stages are usually of fixed duration, not so closely regulated by temperature.

The normal processing of all film types is designed to treat the emulsion of the film as gently as possible, hence the constant temperature. The final image quality rendered by negatives depends, to a great extent, on the behavior of the light-sensitive particles of silver. If they are treated gently with even temperature and minimal soaking time, the tiny particles will remain uniform and only as densely layered as needed. If they are treated harshly, as with uneven chemical temperatures and prolonged soaking, the particles will move about and clump together. This will result in images that appear "grainy" when enlarged. The appearance of too much grain prevents the objects in the picture from assuming their own unique textures. Grainy images seem to have a single texture that differs only in terms of light and dark. At times this may be a desirable quality. If so, then the photographer will break the rules of film processing and intentionally produce a grainy image.

After the film is immersed in wetting agent, a solution that prevents the formation of water spots, it is removed from the reel and hung to dry, using clips or clothes pins, one clip to hold it and a second attached to the end as a weight.

Depending on the heat and humidity of the drying area, the film should be allowed to dry for 1 to 2 hours. Be careful to prevent dust from settling on the wet film, and avoid excessive handling while the film is wet. Until it dries, the emulsion is soft and highly susceptible to scratches and abrasions.

When the film is completely dry, it's ready to proof. If it's not to be proofed immediately, it should be laid out, emulsion side (dull side) up on a clean, dry work surface and cut into sections that match the length of storage strips.

Making Proof Sheets

Proof sheets, or contact sheets, will allow you to see your negatives as same-size prints. Simply place your negative strips over photo paper and expose the paper through the negative. The proof or contact sheet (the negatives came in contact with the paper) will allow you to see your negatives in the form of prints.

With miniature negatives, such as the 35mm variety, you will examine your proof sheets to determine which negatives, if any, you want to enlarge. A large format negative, like one that is 4 × 5 or 8 × 10 inches, might simply be contact printed.

As with your pinhole images, you will use a sheet of glass or a contact printing frame to make contact prints and proof sheets. For the best results and ease of use, try a wooden printing frame.

Making Prints by Enlarging Negatives

THE ENLARGER

The enlarger is the technical workhorse of the darkroom. Most prints, black and white or color, are made through the enlarging process.

BASIC EQUIPMENT FOR ENLARGING AND PRINTING BLACK AND WHITE IMAGES

- condenser enlarger
- enlarging lens
- negative carrier
- enlarging timer
- grain magnifying focusing aid
- enlarging easel
- multiple contrast printing filters

The processing equipment you already have for photograms and pinhole work will serve for enlarging. Color printing requires some additional equipment

EQUIPMENT FOR COLOR PRINTING

- heat absorbing glass for enlarger
- print processing drum
- color printing filters
- color correction viewing filters

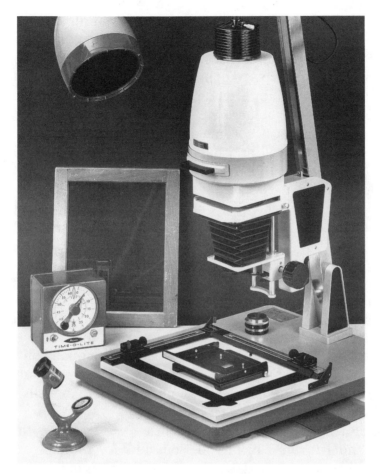

Here is the basic equipment for enlarging negatives: a contact printing frame, enlarging timer, grain magnifier, printing easel, condenser enlarger, negative carrier, enlarging lens, and multiple contrast filters (right side of enlarger baseboard).

Enlarging is like taking pictures in reverse: instead of focusing on an object and letting light in, we project a light image on to paper. As when we use a slide projector, images increase in size as we increase the distance of the negative from the printing surface.

There are two types of enlarger, the condenser enlarger and the diffusion enlarger. The condenser enlarger is equipped with condensers, which are a set of lenses located below the light source and above the negative. The condenser lenses direct even light from the source to and through the negative. The older style diffusion enlarger contains a light source in a domed top to reflect diffused light down through the negative. Most newer and smaller enlargers have condensers.

The diffusion enlarger has essentially been replaced by something called a cold light head. The cold light head, which is preferred by many photographers who print in black and white, is a fluorescent fixture that can replace both the incandescent light source and the condenser lenses, converting a condenser enlarger to a diffusion enlarger. The cold light head provides a more even form of diffuse fluorescent light. The resulting image is not quite as sharp and contrasty as that produced by a condenser enlarger, but prints exhibit greater tonal separation and little trace of scratches and nicks on the negative.

Enlargers vary in size according to the film format they are designed to accommodate. Most small and inexpensive enlargers will accept 35mm and 2¼-inch negatives.

When purchasing used equipment, make certain that the necessary condenser lenses, lens boards, and negative carriers (see below) are included or available.

ENLARGING LENS

Enlarging lenses are relatively simple compared to camera lenses. Unlike a camera lens, the enlarger lens doesn't have to contend with objects in space. The enlarging lens need only focus on a flat plane (the negative) and project it to another flat plane (the paper print to be). Therefore, the enlarging lens requires fewer lens elements and a manually operated aperture to control the volume of light. Depth of field is a more subtle issue in the business of enlarging. The less complicated enlarging lens is generally much less expensive than a camera lens.

Enlarging lenses are generally purchased separately, although some enlarger manufacturers can provide lens kits for their product. Lenses vary in quality and focal length. All enlarging lenses can be used on both condenser and diffusion enlargers. 35mm negatives require a 50mm enlarging lens. 120 film (2¼ inches) requires a 75mm or 80mm lens. The 75 to 80mm lens can also be used to print smaller 35mm negatives. The optics of any enlarger or camera is the most important aspect of the tool. Purchase an enlarging lens that is equal in quality to the lens (or lenses) of your camera. A good lens on your camera will count for little if the lens that enlarges the negative is of poor quality.

Enlarger lenses are generally mounted on a lens board. Lens and board are then attached to the enlarger. When you buy your enlarger, you will also buy a lens board. In some instances, the lens board will need to be drilled with a hole of the proper size. The sizes of most new lenses are standardized. With most newer equipment, drilling is not necessary.

NEGATIVE CARRIER

The negative carrier is the device that the negative is placed in so that it can be held flat and in the proper position within the structure of the enlarger. Negative carriers of different enlarger brands are not inter-changeable. Most individual carriers accommodate one film format; an enlarger that accommodates two or three film formats will require as many different negative carriers. A few enlargers have been manufactured with carriers that adjust to different negative formats. New enlargers usu-ally come equipped with at least one negative carrier. If you buy a used enlarger, be sure it includes the negative carrier(s) you need.

ENLARGING TIMER

It is general practice to plug the light source of an enlarger into a printing timer. The timer takes on the same role as the shutter of a camera. Most newer timers are equipped with mechanisms that are entirely electronic. Other timers are electric, motor driven, mechanical switches.

Timers allow you to turn the enlarger light on for indefinite periods, as when sizing and focusing an image. They also allow for the timed projec-tion of pure light or a projected image. The timing is usually measured in seconds, but may run longer.

A few enlarger systems have built-in timers. In most cases, timers are not included in the design or purchase of an enlarger. It's usually possible to plug an enlarger into a minute-oriented timer used for film processing.

GRAIN MAGNIFYING FOCUSING AID

A simple tool of great value, the grain magnifier is a focusing aid that allows us to make certain that the image to be printed is sharply focused. Focusing an image with the unaided eye, particularly if one wears glasses or contact lenses, can be difficult. The objective is to make certain that your photographs are printed with the same sharpness that is contained in the negative.

ENLARGING EASEL

The printing easel is a purely mechanical device that holds the printing paper flat and in the proper position. It may also allow you to provide bor-ders and easily proportion and crop projected images. Cropping is the business of editing by elimination: we block unwanted edge-sections of an image by either moving the easel or positioning movable blades over the paper's edges.

Some easels have no blades; they offer fixed picture sizes and propor-tions. There are borderless easels that simply hold paper flat and in the proper position.

The most useful easels for general printing are those with movable cropping blades. There are two-bladed and four-bladed models. Four-blad-ed models are larger, heavier, versatile, and more expensive. Two-bladed models are smaller, lighter, easy to use, and less expensive. You should provide yourself with an easel that accommodates the largest paper you intend to use.

MULTIPLE CONTRAST FILTERS

Multiple contrast filters are designed to be used with multiple contrast printing paper. Filter kits are available from all multiple contrast paper manufacturers. Filters of one brand will work with paper of another brand.

Most enlargers are equipped with a filter drawer located in the light head, above the negative and below the light source. The filters come in sizes and materials that allow for trimming to fit the drawers. Avoid using filters below the lens of the enlarger; these will downgrade the quality of the image being projected.

Some filters are made of thin gel or acetate; others are made of heavier plastic. If filters must be used below the lens, use the thin gels. Thin gels, supported by glass in the filter drawer, are excellent for use in large-format enlargers. For small enlargers that see a lot of use, I recommend the heavier plastic filters.

Considerations for Color Printing

HEAT-ABSORBING GLASS

Enlarger light sources are usually high intensity lamps that produce a lot of heat. Filters and negative carriers are close to the heat source and when the temperature rises, heat-absorbing glass protects them from buckling, sagging, and heat damage during exposure.

PRINT PROCESSING CANISTER

Color printing, like film processing, must be done without the use of safelights. Once exposure is accomplished, the color print paper, like film, must be placed in a processing canister. Print processing canisters operate like film processing canisters: chemicals can be added, agitated, and discarded in normal room light, without exposing the paper.

COLOR PRINTING FILTERS

Printing with color negatives and transparencies requires the use of color filters. Color paper emulsions vary from batch to batch, and color filters allow for flexibility in matching negatives to new formulations of emulsion. The color content from picture to picture varies and color filters establish a normal response to differences in color balance.

COLOR CORRECTION FILTERS

Color correction filters are used to view transparencies and prints in order to determine the exact balance of color filtration to be added or subtracted when printing.

Making Black and White Prints

Making prints is the last phase of the photographic process. It allows us dramatic possibilities for creative interpretation of the images contained on our negatives. The options we have for creating different moods in a single image are almost endless.

Before you begin to make prints you should carefully select the negatives to be printed by consulting your proof sheets. Naturally you want to print the images that appear to be the most interesting, but you also want to use the negatives that represent the best exposures. For example, if there's a choice between two images and one is very dark and dense, and the other is lighter, with plenty of detail, the lighter negative is usually the better choice. A negative that is too dense is hard to print, looks fuzzy, and may be difficult to manage in terms of contrast. Negatives that look too light and lack detail should also be avoided.

The Printing Process

The basic printing process can be divided into three distinct steps: establishing the image and testing for exposure; making an overall exposure to determine the need for a change in contrast and the need for burning and dodging; and making the final exposure with desired contrast, burning, and dodging.

The first step calls for making decisions about size, proportion, possible cropping, and exposure time. With your negative in the carrier, turn on the enlarging light and open the aperture of the enlarging lens to its widest setting so you can see the image clearly. Once the image is focused with the unaided eye you can move the enlarger head up or down and refocus, as needed, establishing the desired image size on the printing easel. You can set the exact proportions of the image and crop, if need be, using the blades of the easel or by moving the easel itself. Now you can use the grain magnifier to check the sharpness of the image and make any fine adjustments necessary. With these matters decided, reset the aperture of the enlarging lens to f/8 or f/11 and turn off the light. Set the enlarging timer to 1 second and load the easel with paper. Now you're ready to make an exposure test. Since enlargers have no exposure meters, a manual test is necessary. The results will provide you with an accurate look at a range of exposures from which to choose. This is essentially the same testing procedure used with photograms and pinhole images. Using a sheet of black construction paper, cover all but a ½–inch zone of an unexposed strip of paper (to use a full sheet of paper for a test is a waste of paper) and press the timer button, exposing the zone. Proceed to expose successive zones for 1 second each until you have exposed the entire strip. Now process the test strip using normal time and agitation cycles.

The second step involves making an overall exposure based on careful study of your test. The strip will appear as an image made of graduated segments, from light to dark. A successful test should appear too light at one end and too dark at the other. If the entire test is too dark, close the lens aperture 1 or 2 stops and conduct a new series of exposures on fresh paper. If the test appears too light, redo the test after opening the aperture a stop or two. Look for a zone that contains light and dark tones that present your subject as you think it should look. When you find a suitable zone, count the exposed zones from the light side of the paper to the one you've selected. If, for example, the chosen zone is the sixth from the light side, this tells you that 6 seconds of exposure will produce the desired overall exposure. Place a fresh sheet of paper in the easel, set the timer for 6 seconds, and expose the entire paper. Process the paper in the standard way and examine the results in bright room light.

Step three can take you in one of several directions. It's possible that the overall exposure made in step two has resulted in a good print, with all light and dark values properly represented. The contrast—the extremes of light and dark—might not require any adjustment. These conditions might be easily met if your negative was exposed under bright, subdued light, allowing the film to record a full range of useful values. However, this is usually not the case, particularly in bright sunlight or very subdued light.

Variable Contrast Filters

When a change of contrast is in order, turn to your variable contrast filters. Your decision to search for a contrast change may be a result of an error in the first exposure, a lack of suitable contrast in the original scene, or a desire to interpret your print differently.

To increase contrast with filters, use a filter with a higher number. The numbers range from 0 to 5, or 1 to 4, depending on the brand. The higher the number the greater the contrast. If you don't use any filter, the paper will render contrast in the normal range. The numbering system works the same with graded papers. Increasing or decreasing contrast by one number is nearly equivalent to being able to change the exposure of your negative during picture taking by 1 stop in either direction. An increase in one paper grade or one filter grade will produce the equivalent of 1 f-stop of exposure, up or down; this helps explain the numbering system for paper and filters.

Increasing the contrast of prints requires longer exposure times. Lowering contrast may also lower exposure times. Exposure guides for changing contrast are available with most filter kits and graded paper instructions. The most reliable method for changing contrast is to change filters or paper grades and produce a new test strip. Consult the exposure guide for contrast change and new exposure times and open or close the aperture accordingly. If the guide indicates that changing from a normal filter (or none) to the highest contrast generally calls for two times the previous exposure, you can either open the aperture 1 stop or set the timer for 2 seconds instead of 1. Then produce a new test strip. Choose the best zone of exposure, set the new exposure time and make a new print.

Burning and Dodging

Perhaps the most dramatic changes possible in the printing process are the result of burning and dodging. Burning in is the technique of adding light to selected areas of a print. Dodging is the technique of withholding light from selected areas. Burning in makes areas darker and brings out details hidden in the lightest areas of the print. Dodging makes areas of the print lighter, revealing more detail in the shadows.

Dodging local areas of a print is done during the overall exposure. Burning in is accomplished after the overall exposure is completed. The best guide for determining the time necessary to burn and dodge can be found on the test strip. A thorough test strip will reveal the graduated exposures of both the lightest and darkest areas of the picture. For example, a test strip for a landscape with a lot of sky will be made so that both sky and land appear in each strip (the strip is placed parallel to the horizon, with the horizon dividing the test strip in half). The graduating zones of exposure will be made perpendicular to the horizon. Each zone of test exposure will reveal land and sky. The land, which is usually darker, looks good at 4 seconds of exposure. The sky, however, looks good at 8 seconds; the extra exposure has brought out the contrast between what was a light blue sky and white clouds. If we wish the land and the sky to look their

Each zone of this test represents 1 second of exposure. The lighter side represents the least amount of exposure. This test is the basis for selecting an overall exposure time and how much to burn and dodge. Usually tests are made using a strip of paper (test strip) rather than an entire sheet.

best we have a choice to make: produce a single print that requires exposing the entire image for 4 seconds and burn in the sky for 4 additional seconds; or dodge the earth by subtracting 4 seconds while the earth is exposed, for a total of 8 seconds.

The choice between burning and dodging should be determined by how much manipulation is required. Basing the choice on less rather than more manipulation helps insure a natural look for the prints. Still, the choice between burning and dodging can be complicated by complex shapes, like those of trees or buildings on a horizon that overlap an area that must be burned or dodged. For example, you may want to darken or lighten the sky behind the trees or building, but allow the trees and building to remain as they are. To darken the trees and building that overlap the sky would create an unnatural look in the overall lighting of the scene.

Burning and dodging must be accomplished without creating any unnatural shadows or bright areas. Effective burning and dodging are the results of carefully controlled tools and the close examination of exposure tests.

Tools for burning in are like stencils for light. We can begin with our sheet of black construction paper. The straight edge of the black paper is

This entire print has been exposed for 6 seconds. The dramatic sky looks good, but the horizon, water, and man walking dogs on the beach all appear too dark. The lower section of the image looks better when exposed for 3 seconds. The photographer can burn or dodge to gain the best overall results from both exposures.

Both the sky and the lower section of the image receive the ideal treatments by exposing the entire print for 3 seconds and then covering the lower portion while adding 3 seconds of additional exposure to the sky. By keeping the black construction paper moving during the burning in, the photographer creates a gradual tonal transition between sky and water.

ideal for burning in sky above a straight horizon (it will also dodge the land). Punch a small hole in the center of the black paper so you can hold the paper between the print and the enlarger lens and direct a spot of light onto any part of your print. The spot-lit area can be increased or decreased by raising or lowering the black paper. For areas of a print that require a square-shaped spotlight or a triangular spotlight, you can cut a shape for the center of a new piece of paper and use them as needed.

Dodging tools are shapes that block light. Again, you begin with your sheet of black paper, the edge of which will do nicely for dodging areas above or below a straight horizon, or to the left or right of a tall building in your picture. Dodging areas within the borders of your picture will require black shapes cut out and attached to the end of some thin, dark wire. If the end of the wire is looped and pressed together, paper shapes can be inserted between the wire loops as needed. The wire, with a shape on the end, forms a dodging wand for covering the area of the print that you want to dodge.

Part of the technique of effective burning and dodging requires that the burning or dodging tool be kept moving at all times. You must avoid the creation of strange light and dark areas when burning and dodging. Light that you add or subtract must be blended; this is why you must keep your tools moving with a slight fluttering motion, as though you are very nervous.

Burning and dodging will accomplish what your film cannot: it will allow for the restoration of details in both the lightest and the darkest areas of your prints. Neither the camera nor the film can do this. A really good print, color or black and white, is rarely created without burning or dodging. Most of your best pictures will reveal their true content only when you have mastered the art of printing your own pictures.

Additional Reading

Light and Film, Life Library of Photography. Time-Life Books, 1970.

The Print, Life Library of Photography. Time-Life Books, 1970.

The Negative, The New Ansel Adams Photography Series, Book 2, New York Graphics Society Book, Little, Brown and Company, 1986.

The Print by Ansel Adams. The New Ansel Adams Photography Series, Book 3, New York Graphics Society Book, Little, Brown and Company, 1987.

The New Zone System Manual by White, Zakia, and Lorenz. Morgan & Morgan, Inc., 1978.

8 | What Every Photographer Should Know

An interesting photograph usually contains a number of conventions. In this close-up, Sara Beugen faces strong incandescent side lighting in a dramatic self-portrait. Light from the side reveals the finely sculpted features and textures of her face and hair. *Photo by Sara Beugen*

Basic Photographic Conventions

Photography is a constant series of visual adventures. Whatever the scope or mode of travel, the trip, voyage, flight, drive, walk, or hike is half the fun. I rarely know how far I'll have to travel in my search for an image, or exactly what I'm looking for, but I usually know it when I see it.

I also know that once I've found it, I'll have the familiar elements of time, light, and space to work with. These natural friends are constants in an ever-changing visual world. It's comforting to know that these familiar and universal elements provide certain conventions that are at my disposal, free of charge. As one image seeker to another I would like to introduce you to the conventions that every photographer comes to rely on.

It doesn't matter whether you go out and seek pictures or stay in and build pictures. It matters not what tastes and sensibilities you bring with you or develop along the way. The conventions will serve you well!

The following projects that accompany each convention are offered as a means of becoming familiar with the skills photographers need to master. On another level the conventions represent a shooting script for approaching photographic subjects.

The conventions take the form of situations or environmental conditions that exist, or are created, when photographing. In some instances they are physical relationships that a photographer will recognize and wish to take advantage of, such as a favorable lighting situation, or the advantage of a particularly unique vantage point from which to take a picture.

As tools for creating the most interesting images possible, the conventions are procedures and possibilities for bringing as much visual interest to the intended image as possible. The list reminds us of the fundamental directions we can take and helps us to visualize related possibilities.

The skills required to make judgments that will result in images that meet our requirements are interconnected in complex ways that require us to make choices. With a thorough grounding in the possibilities and enough experience, the difficult problems posed by light, space, time, and motion can be solved.

As we explore the list, it will soon become apparent that items are usually paired in terms of opposites, dual directions, or extremes. It's exciting and reassuring to know that this universal condition—the give-and-take of opposites—is part of the dynamic nature of photography.

To help you solve problems and develop a personal vision, the list of conventions is followed by some corresponding projects. The projects contain pertinent technical data—camera controls, optical aids, and tools—closely associated with each convention. This data, when used in conjunction with technical references for detailed study, should provide a firm basis for acquiring information as you need it.

The list of conventions and their respective projects also will teach you a full working vocabulary of photographic ways and means, but the ultimate goal is for you to develop an informed personal vision. Regardless of your preferences for subject matter, the convention projects will help fill out your photographic experience.

THE SHORT LIST OF CONVENTIONS

Light	*Space*	*Time/Motion*
side lighting	close-up	stop action
back lighting	panoramic space	capturing motion
silhouette	near/far	panning
light from below	natural and man-	creating motion
strobe/electronic flash	made perspective line	multiple exposures
mixed light	bird's eye view	
low level light/night light	worm's eye view	
incandescent light	ambiguous space	
shadows and reflections	soft focus	

Light

SIDE LIGHTING

Side lighting is, quite simply, light that strikes a subject from the side. Side lighting bathes a subject in full highlight-to-shadow detail. The light may be natural (sun or moon), or artificial (incandescent or electronic). Side lighting emphasizes value change by presenting objects in the round, making them appear three-dimensional, as opposed to a silhouette, which looks flat.

Side lighting is the favorite light of any photographer who wants to reveal physical form and texture. Dawn and dusk pictures reveal the topography and material of landscape and architectural forms. Electronic flash or incandescent (photo floods) light aimed from the side illuminates smaller scale forms as effectively as daylight.

The contrast created by some forms of direct side lighting can be softened by adding additional light, or reflecting the side lighting to create secondary light sources. Light added to reveal shadow detail is called fill light. When side lighting dominates, however, physical form and texture is effectively revealed.

Photo Sculptor

Using a model or still life setup, light the subject from a variety of side-oriented directions. Using a single light source, aim the light to stream across the subject, illuminating forms and textures. Record as wide a variety of images as possible. The objective is to create renditions of the same scene that are as different from one another as possible, without changing the position of the camera or the object(s); only the position of the single light should change.

When you've exhausted the broad possibilities of a single light source on your subject, add a second light. Try a dimmer bulb, or keep the second light farther from the subject, aiming it at the shadow side. Create variations of shadow that range from light shadow to deep shadow. This relationship between the relative intensity of two or more light sources is referred to as the lighting ratio. In portrait photography a lighting ratio of 3:1 is often considered ideal. This means that the light on the bright side of the subject is three times brighter than on the shadow side. Various lighting ratios can be arranged and measured with an exposure meter. Move the lights close to or away from the subject, depending upon your choice of a dominant light source.

Instead of adding a second light, use some reflected light bounced on to the dark side of the subject. Bounce the light using white cardboard or cardboard covered with aluminum foil. Change the lighting ratio between direct and reflected light by moving the reflector closer or farther away from the subject.

If you're using color film, try placing transparent color material between the light source and the subject. Also, cover the reflector panels with solid colors. These techniques will add interesting color overlays to the subject.

An interesting catalog of lighting effects can be made quickly with instant print films.

Technique

Accurate light readings, taken from middle gray, represent the primary technical challenge. Use a gray card, or take exposure readings from the lightest and darkest areas of the scene and arrive at an average. A solid average exposure will insure the fullest possible tonal rendition of the scene.

A contrasting background will help you define a form lit by side lighting.

BACK LIGHTING

Back lighting is simply a primary light source located somewhere behind the subject. Such lighting can offer dramatic illuminated edges and often produces reflected light that casts the subject in a combination of simple shape and sculptural form. Middle gray and shadow detail must be maintained in most backlit situations.

Back to Back

Try making a backlit image indoors with bright sunlight coming from a window or door behind the subject. If enough light is bouncing around the room you'll have a combination of side lighting and silhouette. The trick is to prevent the subject from becoming a dark shape.

Technique

The key to using back lighting is making sure your light meter measures middle gray tones in the intended scene. Do not take the light reading by pointing the meter or camera into the brightest light.

In this close-up portrait, soft reflected frontal lighting illuminates the face, in sharp contrast to the intense back lighting that silhouettes a mantle of richly textured hair. The overall effect is one of gentle drama.   *Photo by Justine Van Straaten*

THE SILHOUETTE

A silhouette is the dark, seemingly flat shape of an object, or objects, lit from behind, such as trees and mountains against the sky at sunset or sunrise. The objective is to seek, or create, an interesting silhouette—one that projects interesting shapes or shapes characteristic of familiar objects like human figures. Any opaque object against a bright background can be turned into a silhouette. The otherwise three-dimensional objects will be rendered as flat, solid black shapes. It is also possible to have silhouettes in a portion of a photograph, leaving the remaining area in full light or partial light; this combination will further intrigue the viewer.

Metamorphosis

The goal is to create a series of images, each interesting in its own right, that portray a visually logical metamorphosis. Instead of a caterpillar turning into a butterfly, you might have a teapot turn into a skull or head. Using a highly recognizable object such as a teapot, create a series of silhouette

By dramatically underexposing these objects against a light background the photographer presents a metamorphosis in the form of silhouettes: a woven basket changes in stages to a cow's skull. Part of the skull and a second basket are combined to create the illusion of change. Many more stages of subtle change could be added.

images that depict a metamorphosis from one form to another. Begin by determining the most characteristic shape the teapot can assume and take the first picture. (Remember, you're creating a silhouette, not a fully lit object.) Then turn the first object to create a less characteristic view and place another suitable object into the picture area. By suitable, I mean one that has something of the character of the first object as well as the third or final object. In this case we're looking at round masses with various kinds of bumps and protrusions. Arrange the two objects in such a way that their silhouettes are combined to form a more complex silhouette. One that looks increasingly more like the third and final object, in this case, the skull or head.

This image-building process can take on surrealistic over-tones and be extended by any number of continuous steps and transformations.

In Great Shape

Using a combination of real figures and objects, it's possible to create complex silhouettes that play tricks with scale and real-ity: distant human figures mixed with nearby toy and stuffed animal figures, or miniature human figures mixed with small objects are fun to combine in scenes using exposures designed for creating silhouettes.

Quick Change

Combine a silhouette with an image in full light. This combi-nation is interesting, in part, because it's disorienting. It is accomplished most easily using a combination of natural and artificial light. The most direct way to represent this dual light mode is to put objects or a figure in front of the primary light source and include *a good deal* more of the surrounding scene that is lit by the same source. Another way to create this unusual condition is to project (flash) or reflect light into the foreground of a scene that is in silhouette. You can also block some of the light on the scene in full light and create the sil-houette in what would otherwise be the shadow area. Yet another possibility is to use a reflected image from glass, water, or a mirrored surface. One or the other lighting condi-tion can appear in the form of a reflected image.

Technique

Silhouettes are often created by accident when figures against a bright sky are underexposed because the exposure reading ignored the darker figure. The error suggests the method: for an intentional silhouette, take an exposure read-ing from the bright background, making certain that the fig-ure or objects in the darker foreground are purposefully and dramatically underexposed.

The depth of field encompassing the object(s) in silhou-ette, should be as complete as possible. This will help insure a well-defined shape. A fast shutter speed or electronic flash can be used to light a flat background. When possible, pro-vide even lighting in the background.

LIGHT FROM BELOW

Light from below is often disorienting. Witness the aquarium fish that swims sideways when the light from the front of the tank is stronger than the light from above. We are accustomed to light from the side and light from above; light from below is unusual. The old flashlight-held-at-the-chin ploy, played out in darkness, is always a scary trick. The upside-down light causes the familiar to look strange. A dance floor lit from underneath is the ultimate surreal disco (remember disco?) environment: all the shadows are up instead of down.

The Underworld

Use artificial light to illuminate a scene or still life from below. A human figure or face will add an eerie appearance with light from below. The general effect is theatrical, like the footlights of a stage.

Flashlight fright: a light held under the chin in darkness creates a monster face and a familiar scary joke. Jenny Sirkin made this disorienting image using her younger brother and outdoor garden lighting.   *Photo by Jenny Sirkin*

Technique

If you want your final image to have some gray, take an accurate average exposure reading. If you want the highest possible contrast, take the exposure reading from the brightest parts of the scene, as you would with a silhouette.

STROBE/ELECTRONIC FLASH

Using electronic flash is standard practice for many photographers, even in daylight conditions. A battery powered flash is the most portable form of artificial light. The use of flash has many advantages, including lighting scenes where little or no light is present, freezing motion, and adding fill light to bright daylight. Light from electronic flash can be harsh if pointed directly at a subject. It can appear softer and more natural when it is bounced off a ceiling or wall.

Harsh Reality

Harsh light and outlining shadows are primary characteristics of direct flash. Use the flash to create overly harsh and contrasty images with overly dramatic shadows and reflective surfaces that bounce glaring light back at the camera. Get a little too close to the subject; blow it away with too much light.

Light On Light

Fill flash is most useful in bright daylight when shadows are most prevalent. Fill flash is designed to illuminate the shadow areas in such a way as to appear to be part of the normal, ambient light—the light created by reflected sunlight. Since electronic flash is color balanced to approximate daylight, fill flash can be used to create ambient daylight.

Bouncing Light

Bounce flash is the technique for softening flash so it appears to be ambient daylight or soft incandescent light. Bounce the light off a ceiling or wall. Make sure that the angle of the bounce is such that the light is not falling behind the subject. The angle that the light strikes the reflecting surface equals the angle of reflection. Adequate space between the camera and the subject will insure that the bounced flash hits the intended target. Aim the bounce flash at a point on the wall or ceiling that is halfway between camera and subject.

Just another pretty face? This close-up illustrates the fine detail and harsh shadow that accompanies the use of direct electronic flash. The close-up is particularly effective here, considering the distance both the photographer and the viewer might wish to maintain. *Photo by Matt Olins*

Technique

The essence of using strobe is to forget the usual range of shutter speeds. Use the designated flash synchronization speed that is part of your camera's shutter control dial.

Adjust the camera aperture according to the distance from the subject. Subject distances and aperture settings are calibrated by setting ASA values on the exposure control dial of the flash unit. Finally, it is important to understand the effects of reciprocity failure when using strobe and also when using exposure times longer than 1 second (see the discussion of low level light techniques later in this chapter).

When flash is bounced, it is necessary to open the aperture an extra stop or two. When light is bounced, some is absorbed by the surface it's bouncing off of. To compensate for the loss of light, the aperture must be opened wider than normal.

MIXED LIGHT

This convention calls for the use of more than one type of primary light source in the same image. Use a combination of electronic flash and daylight, or flash and incandescent, or daylight and incandescent or fluorescent light. The technical challenge is to balance the two light sources, producing good exposure in both areas of lighting.

Light Extensions

Balance the light of two sources: outdoor daylight and indoor flash or incandescent with the aid of flash. A person or object inside but next to a window can be made to appear as bright as the scene outdoors. You can bridge the gap between indoor and outdoor light.

A New Light

Create an unusual mood by mixing indoor light sources, including fill flash, with outdoor light or night scene lighting. Add to this automobile lights and strong light coming from different directions. The resulting image will likely appear surreal. Don't be concerned about balancing light in these situations; experiment with direction and different types of light-

The sources of light for this portrait are something of a mystery. There are at least two types of lighting that enliven the image: one is the fading light of the setting sun bouncing off windows and other reflective surfaces, and the other is street lighting from powerful mercury vapor lamps. The mixed light creates an unusual mood that appears to be changing as we view the image. *Photo by Meredith Kamuda*

ing. The fascinating aspect is that familiar environments can become quite unfamiliar!

Technique

Using the outdoor light as the unalterable standard, calculate the flash, or combined incandescent and flash, to match the camera settings required for proper exposure of the outdoor light. It really helps if the flash unit has a feature that manually controls the power output.

The indoor-outdoor relationship may require considerable depth of field; a wide angle lens will help.

When using flash indoors, be careful not to bounce the flash back at the camera when the camera is aimed at a glass window or mirror. Aim the flash from the side, or bounce it off the ceiling.

LOW LEVEL LIGHT/NIGHT LIGHT

Photographing in low levels of light, indoors or outdoors, represents the subtle side of photography. Dramatic, night-lit cityscapes, mood-inspiring interior images, and soft portraits in faint light call for patience and a steady camera. The results, however, are worth the long exposures.

Edge of Day and Night

Photographing a scene lit by city lights and the fading light of day, night lights, or moonlight is a challenge. Nighttime scenes look very different in daylight. Your home and its immediate surroundings photographed at night, with house lights on and street or yard lights ablaze, can appear quite dramatic. Many civic monuments, outdoor sculpture, and points of interest are lit up in interesting ways at night; make pictures of them.

Technique

Making exposures using low levels of available light requires an understanding of the nature of reciprocity failure. Failure to understand this technical phenomenon is responsible for a great many underexposed negatives, even when it seems that you did everything right. Exposures in excess of 1 second or faster than 1/1,000 of a second (strobe) causes film emulsion to behave differently when developed. Expecting the usual reciprocal action between exposure and development will require extra exposure when exposing film and longer development during processing. Take pictures outside, at night, using available street lighting. They will require total depth of field. The goal is to use long exposures, with the aid of a reciprocity failure chart. Such charts are included with directions for exposing and processing film.

INCANDESCENT LIGHT

Light bulbs create illumination by burning a filament. Incandescent (yellow-orange) light is different from daylight (blue), flash (blue), and fluorescent illumination (green); each creates different types of gray tones in black and white photography. Incandescent light usually appears soft and warm. The glowing filament gives off a good deal of red and yellow light that translates into soft gray tones in black and white photos.

Bare Bulb

Use a light bulb or photo floodlight as your only light source, to create a portrait image using hands, feet, a strong arm or graceful neck—anything but a face.

Some images are discovered, others are created. Every element of this carefully constructed photograph is under control. Warm incandescent candlelight provides the ultimate in flattering illumination. Costume and props are carefully selected. All combine to make romance come alive. Sensitive film, careful exposure readings, and extended exposure time make it happen. *Photo by Amanda Perry*

Technique

Depending on the intensity of the light source, you may need to use long exposures with a tripod and small aperture for depth of field. A soft focus image with narrow depth of field might also complement the warm light to create a very warm image.

SHADOWS AND REFLECTIONS

Shadows and reflections exist in many pictures. In the next project they will provide the dramatic subject of your photograph.

Mirror Image

Find the largest mirror you can and use it to create confusion. Facing mirrors provide the image that continues to recede to

The world is turned upside down in this mood-inspiring reflection of trees and sky trapped in a puddle. Real-life reflections usually appear brighter than they really are; extra care should be taken to insure accurate exposure. Depth-of-field calculations are also tricky for mirror images. Nicole Dehne treats the reflected image as real space and provides the necessary aperture and focus settings, recording all the desired details. Photo by Nicole Dehne

infinity, reminiscent of *Alice In Wonderland*. A three-sided mirror (like the ones in the clothing stores) offers interesting possibilities.

Window Shopping

Reflections in store windows offer wonderful overlapping images, combining the worlds that exist on both sides of the glass. The resulting images are complex and often contain the image of the photographer.

Super Imposition

Projected patterns of light and shadow create dramatic images that make us acutely aware of lighting and its power to transform and reveal form. Light, superimposed in random patterns on scenes, mirrors, and objects creates dramatic images of surreal intensity. Light patterns projected over objects and scenes that conform to the general contours of the subject, can reinforce the physical form of the subject.

The projected patterns of light that fall on this baby are usually reserved for mature faces and figures. A chance encounter between strips of sunlight, a playful tot, and the photographer's wry sense of humor all contribute to the final image. She was careful to avoid taking exposure readings from the brightest light.   *Photo by Bibi Tucker*

Use a slide projector and make special pattern images for projection.

Technique

Using mirrors and reflective surfaces is not as easy as it may seem. Images in mirrors require attention to depth of field as well as exposure. Reflections from water and mirrors usually appear brighter than they are. Squint at the scene to see the breakdown of light and dark areas; reflections will subside dramatically when you squint.

Space

CLOSE-UP

Too often, extraneous material is included in a picture. The close-up brings the photographer (and the viewer) closer to a particular subject than might be expected. At times the close-up can generate feelings of discomfort, much like bumping into a stranger. The frame is filled with a form, or part of a form; intimacy mixes with surprise.

Close-ups are usually taken with normal or wide-angle lenses, and they lack depth of field because the lens is brought too close to the subject for anything but the narrowest plane of focus to register. The lack of depth of field indicates a true close-up. The photographer has taken the camera into the face, so to speak, of the subject, and it looks just as it would if we went up close without a camera—mostly blurry.

Telephoto lenses take us up close, but they also flatten an image and often contain more depth of field. This is not a true close-up. It's a magnification, a tightly framed telephoto image.

Macro lenses, or normal lenses on a bellows, can magnify small objects and fill the frame of our cameras and our negatives, but these too are magnifications and the photographic genre is called macro photography.

A Portrait of Parts

Produce a portrait made of close-ups of eyes, nose, mouth, ears, etc. The portrait may take the form of several, or many separate, pictures. Or it might take the form of a photo montage, or a collage mixed with photo paper exposed to produce different values. Another direction is to take the separate images of eyes, nose, and mouth and tape them to the real face and photograph the combination.

Turning Space into Pattern

Close-ups of smaller objects like flowers, shells, and frost on windows reveal not only the intricate forms of tiny natural sculpture, but also the hazy, nebulous shapes of a background. This dramatic difference between something sharp and close and something in the background so out of focus, lends new meaning to the terms "background" and "foreground." The abstractions that form in the background of close-up photos are unique to photography and mirror actual vision that is unaided by lenses.

Technique

In close-ups, a lack of depth of field and blocked light are both potential problems. Accurate focusing is essential. The use of a tripod can be very helpful.

Macro photography, with a reflex camera, requires either a macro lens or a normal distance lens attached to a rail and bellows. It's also possible to add shallow dish magnification lenses to our normal distance lens. These lenses are similar to filters; adding one or more to your lens will make macro images possible. All of these tools are useful for making slides or copy negatives of small images like postage stamps or tiny drawings, or small objects such as jewelry or fly fishing lures.

PANORAMIC SPACE

"Panoramic" suggests space that is deep and wide. A view of a city skyline from a great distance, or looking into the Grand Canyon from the edge are examples.

The Big Picture

Make a picture of great space. Choose the broadest and deepest space possible. The challenge is that the illusion of deep space is not always easily captured. We need clues that allow us to recognize the vast scale contained in the scene. Clear or mixed atmospheric conditions such as distant clouds, fog, and approaching storms provide a sense of great and recognizable scale. Architecture, highways, rivers, bridges—all speak of great spaces when dwarfed by vast space. Occupying a high vantage point is a great advantage but does not guarantee great success. The eye must have real clues to learn the actual scale of the scene.

This dramatic image is the result of mixed lighting and a dynamic near/far stretching of sharply focused space. The figures in the foreground are lit by an electronic flash. The wooded middle ground is in near silhouette while the setting sun illuminates the details of the distant lake and city skyline—achieved with a long exposure and a pop of the flash. *Photo by Josepha Conrad*

NEAR/FAR

Often used by photo journalists as well as landscape and editorial photographers, the near/far convention is a combination of close-in and panoramic view. This convention is a tool used to connect an individual or small object to a larger context or environment. Imagine a close-up of the mayor of a large city, with a characteristic view of the city skyline as a clear background. In landscape work the tool is used to highlight a small form, such as a delicate plant or animal, and relate it to its larger environment: the desert or mountains.

The dramatic spatial pull from foreground to background and back again is a dynamic function that must be carefully controlled. We do not want the eye to disappear into the background and off the picture; the eye must always be led back to the foreground. Strong directional lines and circular paths of interest keep the eye from wandering.

The Spatial Connection

Relate a close-in object to a broader context. Use a person, animal, or object and carefully consider the distant background.

Technique

This convention requires a sharp, close-in image and a reasonably sharp background. Extensive depth of field is essential. A wide-angle lens is the most efficient way to achieve the effect. For the most dramatic spatial effects from this convention, use a pinhole camera.

NATURAL AND MAN-MADE PERSPECTIVE LINES

Natural or man-made perspective lines, like a river that narrows as it reaches the horizon or railroad tracks that disappear into the distance, make dramatic spatial statements. These are physical elements that we can relate to in terms of their size and scale. When they become the subject of a picture or play a role in leading the eye to a desired point of interest, space becomes a dynamic force on a panoramic scale.

Drawing the Lines

Use side lighting to illuminate the landmarks and textures of a landscape and define the space. This will reveal the width and breadth of your scene.

The space-defining perspective lines of a white winter road cut through the dense texture of woods edged in snow. The meandering borders of the tree lines that straddle the road are mirrored in the arcing branches that meet at the horizon. Streaks of gray on the well-traveled road pull the eye to a distant speck—a car or a figure—then up to a patch of sky that meets the tops of trees. Then the eye's journey begins anew. *Photo by Nicole Dehne*

Technique

A wide-angle lens helps to take in the scene and create the illusion of even greater space. Use a tripod for added sharpness and clarity. Haze filters in front of the camera lens can help reduce the effects of atmospheric haze that may obscure important detail. Absolute depth of field is essential. When the closest object in your intended scene is off in the distance, simply focus the camera at infinity.

BIRD'S EYE VIEW

This convention is used to photograph subjects from a higher-than-normal point of view. Normal means somewhat higher than a simple sitting or standing position. It does not refer to pictures taken from an airplane; this is called aerial photography. It also does not mean taking a picture from a high-rise window. This is panoramic photography and it represents a normal view for high-rise dwellers or visitors to the tops of famous skyscrapers. The bird's eye view convention is much more accessible. Standing on a chair or step ladder and pointing the camera down, or holding the camera overhead and aiming down, will provide an effective bird's eye perspective.

A solitary figure appears to question the convenient reordering of perspective adopted by Juliet Graham as she assumes a bird's eye view. Her lofty perch makes a textured background of a brick courtyard. Tree branches in the foreground permeate the image along with a sprinkle of fallen leaves. The flat, graphic mix of natural form and geometric pattern is enhanced by shadowless overcast lighting and complete depth of field. *Photo by Juliet Graham*

The effects are many: the background space is limited, familiar forms appear smaller than usual, the angular point of view highlights new visual patterns, and the familiar takes on new interest.

Looking Down on the World

Make use of the bird's eye view to photograph an individual or small group. By photographing down at the subject, we are able to limit backgrounds that might otherwise prove too deep and distracting. Use the convention to limit space and focus interest on the work or play activity of an individual, or add interest to what might be just another group of friends for the photo album or yearbook.

Technique

The essential idea is to place the camera slightly above the usual standing or sitting eye level. Frame your image carefully and pay special attention to lighting. The wide-angle lens offers advantages in terms of added depth of field and exaggerated distortion from the higher perspective.

WORM'S EYE VIEW

Similar to bird's eye view, this convention is designed to place the familiar in a new and more dramatic perspective—that of the worm. The effects are dramatic: familiar forms appear much larger. Like the bird's eye view, the worm's eye view requires a subtle shift away from normal points of view like sitting or standing. Worm's eye view is the equivalent of taking a position lying on the ground. Placing your camera on the floor and aiming upward is a workable approach. Your goal is to lend a new look to the familiar. And this is the way to make a short person appear taller.

Looking Up

Make a small child appear large and threatening. Make a picture from the point of view of a pet about to receive a dog biscuit. The idea is to take maximum advantage of the low-down perspective.

Technique

Adequate depth of field and careful framing are essential. A wide-angle lens is very helpful. A pinhole camera will provide the greatest drama in terms of space and relative scale.

From this worm's eye view a figure looms above us in dramatic fashion. Side lighting, the frozen motion of billowing hair, and the soft-focus of tree branches enhance the suspenseful quality of the image.   *Photo by Josepha Conrad*

AMBIGUOUS SPACE

The name of this convention suggests uncertainty over the nature of the subject due to an unusual perspective or an odd arrangement of familiar objects. Or perhaps the ambiguity is caused by combinations of what appear to be different types or scales of illusionistic space—space created by reflective surfaces or solid surfaces that appear as voids.

Definitely Unclear

Ambiguous space images are usually discovered on the proof sheet rather than the viewfinder. Look over proof sheets and find an interesting image that for some reason is puzzling. One way to proceed is to determine what causes the ambiguity and retake the photo, making changes that you think will enhance the ambiguous nature of the scene. Good examples of this convention usually provide the viewer with clues as to the actual nature and source of the image.

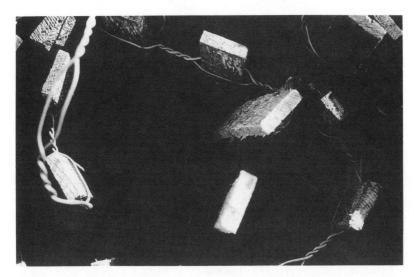

Because the subject of this close-up is ambiguous, the image appears quite abstract. Jon Morris' eye for detail discovers the top of a rolled-up snow fence raked by early morning light. The linear wire sections and textured wood lath establish visual themes that hold our interest. *Photo by Jon Morris*

Technique

A photographer's introduction to ambiguous images is usually prompted by mistakes and unintentional exposures. We see examples of ambiguous images on proof sheets, and more often than not we don't remember taking the picture. We see unusual compositions that may be interesting, unfamiliar image-framing that defies our usual habits, or we discover partial images and physical vantage points that, at first viewing, seem totally unrelated to our experience. But images that hold our interest offer clues to understanding what we see, and we decide to either forget the image or explore it further. We may, with minor adjustments, retake the image, making a conscious effort to retain the unusual aspects and provide clues that are not so subtle. In this way we learn to make interesting images from the most casual of circumstances.

SOFT FOCUS

Soft images depicting dream-like spaces are well within the sphere of authentic photographic qualities. While complete depth of field is often valuable, images that are soft or blurry represent highly realistic representations of movement and what might be termed shifting vision: the act of changing focus, the time between sharp focus on one scene and refocusing on another. Time and movement are both involved, for movement requires time. The blurry image is restless, impatient, and evokes a sense of jarring realities and shifting attention. At its most sedate, the soft image provides us with an impression; it reminds us of the fleeting moments when all we can remember are distant thoughts.

Art or Error

Making the image out of focus and showing movement via slow shutter speed leaves everything in the image looking somewhat fuzzy. The trick is to make the movement appear intentional. The difference between this project and creating motion is one of degree. In this case we desire subtlety.

Creative Mess

Using a clear (UV) filter smeared with a thin (very thin) coating of petroleum jelly such as Vaseline you can proceed to

This bicycle seems lifted from a dream. The suggestion of overall motion is the result of a slow shutter speed. The blur is similar to the sensation that occurs when we shift our gaze from one scene to another. The softness of the image may also be enhanced by focusing on a point too far away or too close to the center of activity. Photographs made with soft-focus techniques often suggest a dreamlike state. *Photo by David Wan*

take pictures as usual. Try portraits using this technique. Also, try smearing the jelly from the outer edge of the filter toward the center, leaving the center free of jelly. The goal is to create an image that gets progressively fuzzier from center to edge.

Cover Up

Use a "scrim" of translucent texture between the lens and the subject to create a different kind of fuzz. Try some gauze or lace held close to the camera lens, focusing on an image as you normally would. Seeing a sharp image between a fuzzy grid of haze, in regular patterns, creates an interesting in-focus, out-of-focus texture.

Technique

A good deal of experimentation is required with shutter speeds, sharp focus, and depth of field when the camera is moving. Smearing filters with petroleum jelly helps to provide maximum depth of field. When experimenting with scrim materials, begin by using the camera on a tripod.

Time/Motion

STOP ACTION

Freezing a moment in time represents the essence of most photographic images, and stopping the action is one of the major achievements of camera and film. The primary control is the shutter, set to a fast speed (250-1,000+). The surest way to use this convention is to photograph someone or something defying the laws of gravity. Stop them, or it, in midair, no blur, free of fuzz, clean and sharp. It's possible to use a flash to gain similar results, but only where the light is limited. Try using available light and the fastest shutter speed possible. Make certain there is enough light and adequate depth of field.

Defying Gravity

Photograph figures defying the law of gravity by dancing or engaging in sports activity. Ballet, gymnastics, skateboarding, track and field—all the activities we see documented in the arts magazines and sports news.

Bright daylight and sensitive film allowed Josepha the use of fast shutter speeds (⅟₅₀₀ of a second or faster) and small aperture settings (f/11 or smaller). The results: motion is stopped, and extreme depth of field encompasses the action and the space around it.   *Photo by Josepha Conrad*

Shapes in Space

Mix the stop-action convention with that of making effective silhouettes of figures engaged in the act of escaping the forces of gravity.

Technique

Shutter speed is the prime factor, along with adequate lighting and depth of field.

CAPTURING MOTION

Capturing blurs of motion is another accomplishment of the photographic process. The image, however, should not be so blurry that the viewer cannot identify the moving subject. There should be enough detail for the viewer to determine the general nature of the subject's activity. The non-

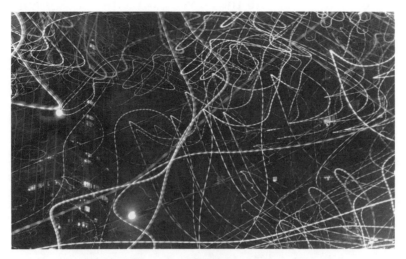

Secured firmly on a tripod, the camera captures the movement of a string of pulsing decorative lights blown about by the wind. Note the stable image of a high-rise building and bright stationary lights in the scene's left side. The shutter is open for nearly a full second, the aperture is open wide, and the lens is focused at infinity.   *Photo by Ethan Steinberg*

moving segment of your picture will stand out in sharp, clear, and unmoving contrast to the fast-moving blur.

Point/Counterpoint

Capturing motion is a fine example of point/counterpoint: a comparison of static object and moving object, two states of motion, one enhancing the other. Dramatic action isn't required, just a central image that is in motion, motion that isn't too abrupt—perhaps a pet dog jumping for a snack held up high.

Technique

With camera held still, preferably on a tripod, set the proper shutter speed (1/4 to 1/30) to allow a blurred image to form on the film. Aside from using the proper shutter speed, adequate depth of field and good subject/background contrast (white against black, etc.) are important technical factors.

PANNING

Panning consists of taking a picture of a moving object by following its motion with the camera and making an exposure during the synchronized movement. The use of slower shutter speeds (1/4 through 1/30) makes the panning effect possible. The end product is an image that appears to allow the viewer to move along with the subject, while the background whizzes by in a blur.

Moving Along

A runner, bicycle rider, skateboard jockey, and other moving bodies can provide a suitable subject for panning. The most dramatic images will result from those instances when we can get reasonably close to the moving subject. The closer we are to the subject, the more dramatic the effect of moving background behind a fairly well-defined subject.

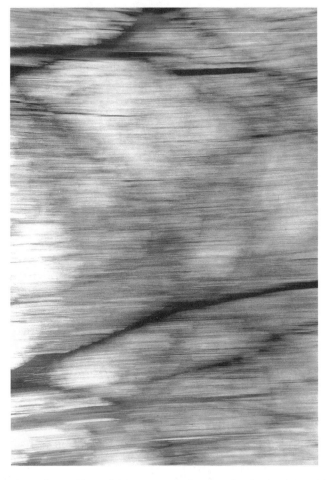

Panning captures the motion of the camera as it passes by the background. To get this image Nicole Dehne sped under overhanging trees, and we have the feeling of traveling with her. Success is a matter of slowing down shutter speeds and following a subject while making the exposure. Most often the photographer runs or cycles and pans the object in front of a background. In this instance, you and I are the subject as we pass under a canopy of wistful branches.   *Photo by Nicole Dehne*

Position yourself so that the moving subject is passing directly across your line of sight, perpendicular to your angle of view. As the moving subject approaches your position, twist to keep the moving subject in your line of sight and follow its movement as it passes you. While following the action of the subject, trip the shutter of the camera, continuing to move in sync with the subject. You can combine this action with a bird's or worm's eye view to add extra spatial drama.

Technique

Proper shutter speed is the most important element. Some trial and error will be necessary. The faster the moving object, the faster the shutter speed you will need; the shutter, however, must always be set to a relatively slow speed: 1/30 to 1/4 of a second. Depth of field should be set to include objects in the background. If the depth of field is not sufficient, there will be no detail in the whooshing motion of the background, and the viewer will not be able to distinguish the subject from the background.

CREATING MOTION

Creating motion where none exists is possible by moving the camera during a slow exposure time. The "earthquake" effect is accomplished by jarring the camera while the shutter is open.

Earthquake

Locate a scene that appears placid, static, and otherwise unmoving. An urban scene might produce a dramatic image.

Technique

Use a tripod or set the camera down on a stable surface and compose the image. Set the shutter speed to the slowest setting that can be used with an aperture that provides as much depth of field as possible. Then, trip the shutter with a cable release. During the exposure, give the camera a sharp bump, just enough to move it slightly. Combine this convention with long exposure and the use of a flash for an image that contains multiple forms of movement. The camera is best used on a tripod. Again, depth of field, high subject/background contrast, or points of dramatic light, combined with the right jarring action, will create the illusion of dramatic motion.

MULTIPLE EXPOSURES

Multiple exposures often occur accidentally when a camera fails to advance film properly and the exposed images overlap. The resulting transparent overlapping represents a form of implied motion that defies known conventions of time and space.

Two for One

Try combining two images that are as different as can be, such as a room interior and the image of an aquarium. Or try images that represent two vantage points in the same room or of the same person.

Technique

Many cameras, such as the single lens reflex models, allow us to make multiple or double exposures by pressing the rewind button at the base of the camera body while we cock the film advance lever: the shutter is cocked but the film doesn't advance. The result is two pictures on one frame of film. Treat each exposure as a separate image and avoid, when possible, bright skies that will blacken the negative and prevent transparent overlapping.

The illusion of motion reverberates throughout this panoramic night scene. Sara Beugen placed her camera on a tripod and tapped it sharply during the exposure. The shutter was slowed to accommodate the low light level and to allow for the opportunity to create motion. The aperture is opened wide and the lens, at this great distance, is focused at infinity.   *Photo by Sara Beugen*

This photograph was made using multiple exposures: four overlapping images on the same negative, caught with an electronic flash (the small bright spots on the left that look like a dotted i). By working outdoors, Matt Olins gave himself ample space so the light from the flash exposed only the figure. Overexposure and excess of image-overlap might have been a problem if more ambient light had bounced around in a smaller space. The resulting image is interesting and dramatic. *Photo by Matt Olins*

Additional Reading

Photography, adapted from The Life Library of Photography by Barbara Upton and John Upton. Educational Associates, a division of Little, Brown and Company, 1976.

Dictionary of Contemporary Photography by Leslie Stroebel and Hollis N. Todd. Morgan & Morgan, Inc., 1977.

9 | Color

How would you color this black and white image? Adding color is fun, whether you want it to make the image look real or surreal. The subject photo is a 16 × 20-inch positive enlarged from the original 5 × 7-inch image. The larger size makes for greater visual impact and easier coloring. Here the image is surrounded by coloring media including photo oils, marking pens, and a colored pencil. You can use cotton balls and swabs to apply and blend color pigments and oil-based materials.

Color and the associations we make with the visible elements of the chromatic spectrum are powerful messages. Most photographers, professional and amateur, choose light-sensitive materials that provide color images. Color and light are inseparable, even in black and white photography. Why do so many photographers prefer to work with black and white materials?

The primary reasons have to do with aesthetic choices. Many photographers work in black and white to avoid the all too attractive distractions of color. The presence of color often makes some elements of a picture too important when compared with noncolor-related elements the photographer wants to emphasize. For example, the delicate play of light and shadow streaming through a forest scene might be upstaged by bright green or yellow patches of sunlit grass and flowers. The photographer wants to highlight the total effect of sunlight on the forest environment, not the colorful patches of green and yellow flora.

Color can offer highly symbolic meaning that may have nothing to do with either the photograph's subject or the intentions of the photographer. I've often been struck by the comparison between color scenes of dramatic events and those captured in black and white. If the scene is one of sadness or anguish, the presence of color can belie the emotions. Scenes of poverty-stricken areas often include the brightly colored garments of the poor. A black and white rendition of the scene might be more in keeping with the grim nature of the overall message.

In a more technical vein, black and white materials have generally offered more flexibility when dealing with low light levels and are easier to use when processing. More recently, the gap in technical advantages is narrowing. Color materials have come along that offer increased sensitivity and easier processing.

A difference in cost is often a factor. In general, color materials have been more expensive than those for black and white, especially for the photographer that processes his or her own film and prints. Another long-term cost factor is related to the archival qualities of black and white materials compared to that of color material. Historically, older black and white negatives and prints are generally known for their stable qualities relative to longevity. Color film and print materials that have been around for some time have been known to fade over time. As a result, those who invest in photographic imagery, either as collectors or archivists, have been reluctant to trust color materials to withstand the ravages of time. Again, some newer color materials appear to offer increased resistance to fading and material deterioration. Only with the passage of time will we know for sure how well new materials will survive.

Given the power of color to dominate an image, the aesthetics of working in color must be carefully considered. Professional photographers spend a great deal of time producing color images that are carefully controlled in terms of lighting and accuracy. Flesh tones must be just right and the colors of products must match the original subjects.

Color is also used to alter the familiar and produce dramatically different effects by changing expected color relationships: a purple sky, a green face, and pink trees appear highly unusual.

Achieving accurate color—duplicating the colors of the environment on film and in prints—is the exception rather than the rule. There are many variables to be considered beyond the type and quality of light used. Light-sensitive color materials are complex, light sources emit different colors, lenses vary in the accuracy with which they transmit the colors of the spectrum, and individuals perceive colors differently. Careful inspection and comparison will usually reveal significant differences between picture and subject. Most people who make color pictures are pleased when color rendition provides a close match.

Color Is Relative

Photographers and artists learn that one of the most important aspects of color is that despite strong associations with mood and symbol, despite the ways in which color use is categorized and formulated, colors interact in ways that are quite relative. Individual colors, tints, shades, and hues change depending on how they are combined.

We may think of red as a warm color associated with passion and blue as a cool one, placid in its symbolic nature. But even the most common associations can change drastically when these colors are coupled with other combinations. The same red placed next to green will look quite different next to yellow.

Color Systems and Associations

The organization of the visible spectrum into primary, complementary, analogous, and tertiary colors is useful when mixing colors and devising color schemes. We know that in theory, red, blue, and yellow can be used to mix any complementary or analogous colors we need. We know that the presence of all the colors in the light spectrum results in white light. The presence of all pigment colors results in some form of black. Using bright primary colors together offers clear but separate color effects, as in the flags of nations or competing products on store shelves. We see that a primary color like red clashes with its complementary color green. Combinations of primary and complementary colors, such as red and green, blue and orange, and yellow and purple, are used together when intense, interactive color is desired, as in the uniforms of sports teams or holiday decorations. People build wardrobes around neutral hues and shades that complement their own coloring. Often, we save bright colors, of a complementary nature, for festive occasions. Black, white, and dark blue are used in more formal circumstances. Colors are chosen for both their symbolic value (black is associated with death, white with purity) and for the way they interact with other colors. Intense colors and combinations are used for festive occasions, subtle hues and neutral tones are often the colors we live with on a daily, hourly basis. All of these associations are based in cultural beliefs and they change depending on the culture. The most widely held symbolic associations are probably those associated with the universal natural world. Blue is the color of the sky and sea. Yellow is a universal symbol for the sun and deities, green is symbolic of earthly fertility and abundance. Red is the color of blood and therefore of sacrifice and courage. After the universal associations, what do we have left? An infinite variety of powerful visual sensations of a highly experiential and symbolic nature, all of which is relative. Much of it changes minute by minute, renewing itself daily, monthly and yearly in the cycle of the seasons.

Learning to see (I mean really see) color means becoming aware of its constantly changing nature. Learning to make practical use of color relationships, acquiring an awareness of symbolic color, and linking ideas to your personal color sensibilities.

Technique

Like black and white film, color film is not as sensitive as the human eye. The decisions we make when exposing color materials must be even more accurate in terms of what we wish to represent in the picture before us. If your picture contains a full value scale of light and dark, as on a sunny day, you must represent either the light or the dark end of the scale.

Most work with color materials benefits from a narrow range of light-to-dark values. Outdoors, a somewhat overcast sky will reveal more color than a sunny scene. Bright sunlight washes out color by producing too much highlight and shadow contrast.

Side lighting that comes with dawn and dusk is muted compared to the intense light of midday. For this reason, landscape photographers using color material prefer early morning and early evening light; it reveals form and is less intense, providing deeper colors as well as good shadows. The limited value range of the prevailing side light allows more of the brightest and darkest tones and colors to register within the usable sensitivity range of the film.

Color Projects

When we say that something is colorful, what do we mean? Deciding that something is colorful can be very personal. Do we recognize a wide variety of colorful situations and color relationships? Bold color is easy to spot, subtle coloration can be more difficult to recognize.

The objective of the following projects is to seek out and compare a variety of color systems, including images of neutral coloration and black and white images. The act of seeking, identifying, and comparing color systems and situations will help make you aware of color everywhere.

The Color of Time

Compare the color quality of light at sunrise, high noon, and sunset. Choose a clear day and a scene that offers as much panoramic space as possible, along with landscape and cityscape that will reflect the general color of light on the horizon. The idea is to photograph the immediate environment and note the effectiveness of the light and color that define the surrounding landscape.

If the sky is colorful it means that sunlight is passing through atmospheric conditions, such as cloud, fog, haze, smog, or smoke. The old saying "Red sky at morning, sailor take warning" is based on the idea that the sun is shining through distant storm clouds. "Clear sky at night, sailors' delight."

Often, the most dramatically colored skies occur during powerful natural events such as the eruption of a volcano. The sun shining through layers of airborne volcanic ash can make for intense color in skies hundreds of miles from the active volcano.

Such explosive drama isn't necessary to achieve a lively difference in the general effects of sunlight near dawn, dusk, and high noon. The reversal of dramatic shadow patterns evident in the images photographed when the sun is on opposite horizons and the lack of long, defining shadows at high noon tell very different stories in the same scene.

The Black and White of Color

Often the reasons why a scene or object attracts your photographic eye will be a mystery even to you. What you thought was attractive due to color, lighting, or symbolism might have caught your eye for a different reason. This project can sharpen your critical sensibilities which are associated with your initial assumptions about why you're interested in a certain subject. For an eye-opening experience, compare color and black and white photos of the same scene, taken as close together in time as possible.

First, the scenes should attract the eye, for all the usual reasons that motivate us to take a picture: subject, lighting, color, etc. Photograph each pair of images in the same manner, with the camera position and controls set exactly the same.

The most valuable lesson may be to recognize the relative importance that color plays in your choice of subject and imagery. If the photographs remain interesting in black and white, as well as in color, then the combination of pictorial elements that prompted your choice are widespread and not based primarily on color. If the black and white version is of little interest compared to the color rendition, color was the main draw and the element of real interest to you. If the black and white version turns out to be the really strong image, the major attraction was not the color content of the scene; other factors drew your attention. These exercises can help develop greater certainty in your vision. It's often difficult to know if the attraction is color, form, or some more complex content. This exercise will also help you determine the best approach to take in pursuit of your visual ideas. It may be that color is not a necessary ingredient in what you would like to say. Or it may be confirmed that color is the primary concern in your images.

Prime Time Color

Seek a subject rich in primary colors: bright, full-strength reds, yellows, and blues, and little else. Fill the frame with these colors and take pains to purposefully under- and overexpose the images by a stop or two. The exposure experiments will provide you with research material. Color, like values, can be manipulated in ways that offer pleasant surprises, depending upon the subject you've chosen. If the prevailing light isn't to your liking, over- or underexposure may provide the desired results. Do this bit of research for each color project.

Colors that Clash

Find or assemble a scene made up mostly of primary and complementary colors. Remember, the complement of red is green; green is the result of mixing the remaining two primary colors: blue and yellow. Find or use as many primary and complementary sets as possible. The character of a primary/ complementary mix is drastically different from a scene made from primary colors alone. The Indians of the American Southwest are known for the brightly colored woven blankets they craft. Some of the many traditional color schemes they use are made by combining a broad range of bright primary and complementary colors. The name aptly given to this bold style of bright, vivid weaving describes the character of primary and complementary colors used together: they're called eye-dazzlers.

Smooth Color

Use primary and analogous colors to photograph a subject. Any mix of two primaries, red and yellow for example, produces a blend of what is usually harmonious. A combination of red, red-orange, yellow-orange, and yellow appear as a carefully measured blend of two primary colors. Blue and yellow beget green; blue, blue-green, and green harmonize. Red and blue become purple; blue, blue-purple, and purple seem right together. There is no clear-cut primary color separation, no complementary eye-dazzling, just smooth transition from one primary color to another.

Less Is More

Photograph a subject containing neutrals, like black, white, and gray or neutrals with some subtle coloration and a small, but highly noticeable bit of bright color, either a primary or a complementary color. This circumstance represents great drama between neutral values and color; the bit of color becomes very important, whether or not its form or presence is essential. Circumstances like this prompt some photographers to use nothing but black and white film. Such occurrences prompt other photographers to use nothing but color film.

Protective Decoration

Pick a color background and color an object so that it is all but invisible when placed in the picture. Use a human face or portions of a body and stage makeup. Take a group of photos documenting the progress of making the subject disappear into the background. Display the photos in reverse order, beginning with the scene minus the camouflaged subject.

Cam-O-Color

Devise a camouflage pattern that will allow an object to fit into a natural or constructed background. Devise camouflage for everyday settings, like an office, a living room, a cafeteria. Camouflage for the jungle and the desert has already been done. If an individual needs to blend into a white wall with red dots, give him or her a white T-shirt and stick red adhesive dots on the person and the shirt. Place the newly dotted subject in front of the dotted wallpaper, then take the picture.

Color Projection

Use colored lights to change a subject. Colored bulbs, a colored jell over a flash or floodlight, or colored slides projected on a subject or environment will provide a whole new aura to any subject or scene. Use the most unlikely colors on a particular scene to create a surreal atmosphere.

Instant color film is fun to use for viewing changes or to test the effectiveness of your efforts prior to final exposure with film that produces negatives or direct color positives (transparencies).

Hand Coloring Black and White Images

Most hand coloring performed on black and white photographs allows the original photographic image to show through the added color. This means that the coloring material must be transparent. At times, it might be desirable to block much of the original photo image, allowing only portions of it to show through. This requires opaque, or solid color.

You can use a number of different coloring mediums to hand color black and white prints. Sophisticated methods make use of lacquer sprays and airbrushed color dyes. For our purposes, less complicated techniques will do. Colored pencils, markers, and oil color pigments allow for fairly direct application.

A primary consideration is the paper's surface. Some of the easier to use coloring mediums adhere better to dull or semigloss prints than to glossy prints. If hand-coloring is an important part of a project, experiment with suggested coloring mediums on different paper surfaces before producing a lot of prints.

OILS

Perhaps the most versatile coloring medium is oil color formulated for black and white photographs. Photo oils can be purchased at art and photo stores, in small or large sets, complete with special mediums, application tools, and instructions. The oils produce transparent color glazes that allow the tones of the photograph to show through. Working with oil color requires some practice, but before long you will find this method not only serviceable but fun.

MARKING PENS

Marking pens, permanent or water soluble, offer coloring options that include opaque, translucent, and transparent applications. Light colored markers can achieve transparent effects that allow the tones of the photograph to show through. Darker colors will produce a translucent, or opaque appearance. Again, experimentation is the key to success. Begin by bringing sample photo paper to the art supply store (photo stores don't usually sell markers). Apply marker colors to the various paper surfaces. Markers usually leave texture as well as color on the print. Choose a few markers that produce different levels of transparency and opacity, and play with color effects.

PENCILS

Colored pencils should be waxy. They usually require a dull surface so glossy surfaces must be covered with a dulling spray. Pencils allow a lot of control, but are not transparent. Pencil sets offer wide color selection and produce interesting surfaces. As with markers, you should experiment with pencils on paper samples brought to the art supply store. Film marking pencils and grease pencils can be added to the list of possibilities. Try whatever seems waxy or sticky enough.

Additional Reading

Color, Life Library of Photography. Time-Life Books, 1973.

Photographic Color Printing: Theory and Technique by Ira Current. Focal Press, 1987.

Retouching Your Photographs by Jan Way Miller. Amphoto, 1986.

10 | Advanced Projects for Every Photographer

A mild bird's eye perspective coupled with light from an overcast sky produces a softly textured portrait of friends. The view from above limits the depth of the background, keeping our eyes on the subjects. The portrait has a candid quality; everything about the image is relaxing. *Photo by Justine Van Straaten*

The advanced projects that follow invite the full and creative use of all the photographic conventions covered in earlier sections. They also require a heightened sense of the chosen subject and a concentrated effort to establish visual relationships between your individual photographs. Use them to develop your own artistic mark.

Portraiture

Portraits account for the great majority of photographs that have been taken since the invention of photography. Most of the pictures that amateur photographers make are snapshots of other people. Most professional photographers are in the business of photographing people. School photographers record your appearance, along with all your classmates, in a given year. Wedding photographers record the likenesses and formality of a major rite of passage and provide the visual evidence of family history. Fashion photographers help sell clothing and record the styles of a generation. The photojournalist and the newspaper photographer bring us events from around the world and around the corner. Advertising photographers help create enticing lifestyle images. Public relations photographers help all manner of business and governmental entities put their best image forward. Industrial photographers add visual substance to the annual report, and medical photographers record everything medical. They all take pictures of people, but not all pictures of people are portraits.

A snapshot can be as simple as capturing a likeness of someone, the kind that might appear on a driver's license. But how many individuals would like to be remembered the way they usually appear on an ID card? A meaningful portrait is one that reveals something about the subject. A portrait may or may not be particularly flattering, though most conventional forms of portraiture attempt to portray the subject, quite literally, in the best possible light. Good portraiture can provide insight into the real personality and interests of an individual. Basic sensibilities and typical moods can show through. We can receive a real moment in a real life, or a synthetic pose having nothing to with the subject; it's not always easy to tell one from the other.

The goal is to use all the conventions of light, space, time, and motion to make portraits that reveal personality and character. At times you'll want to flatter your subject, at other times, when flattery might do an injustice, you can use the available light of reality. Whatever the purpose, it is good to challenge yourself to get beyond an image that simply looks like the subject.

Self-Portrait

How do we picture ourselves? The challenge of taking your own picture—a revealing portrait—should provide you with some special insight as to how the subject of a portrait feels about having his or her personality on exhibit. Your first response may be to think of ways to make yourself look really good. But what does looking good really mean? Handsome, beautiful, intelligent, witty, taller, shorter, younger, older—all of the above?

You might begin by considering your primary interests. Do you love sports, a hobby, skateboarding, chess, cheerleading—whatever positive image you and others might associate with you is a good place to start.

Do you want to be straightforward about this portrait, or is it in your nature to do the unexpected? A little humor, a lot of humor, perhaps? Ask yourself some serious, or not so serious, questions: What sort of portrait would you make of yourself if you were applying to a college you desperately want to get into, or for a job as a stand-up comic, a bodyguard for your favorite sports personality, a movie star, a soap opera hero or heroine, a high fashion model; the list is endless. The challenge: dare to look different, even if it's just for a laugh. Dare to look serious, especially if you are! Above all, dare to look.

Technique

Taking your own picture with ease depends on your camera. Most newer single lens reflex or range-finder cameras are equipped with a timer. Set the timing mechanism and get yourself in the picture. When you use simple cameras without timers or cable release sockets, the aid of a friend who can trip the shutter may be necessary. If your camera has a socket for a cable release, it is possible to use a long version of this simple but useful tool. Many photographers simply point a hand-held camera into a mirror, which is fun, but too easy. Don't forget the trusty pinhole camera. By the time you slip into the picture, the pinhole will just be getting started exposing the picture. (Remember, take a pinhole photo in bright, natural light.)

Family Portrait

It's time to get the immediate family together and ask them to hold still for a moment. The business of scheduling such an event may be the most difficult part. If scheduling doesn't work, the family portrait may have to take the form of a photo montage—a large image pieced together from several smaller images—and even if everyone can get together, it might be fun to take several prints of the same image and use them to make one montage. Try using several prints from the same negative, making each a different size. Use one print as the main image and paste squares and rectangles cut from the extra prints over the main background photo. You can also mix color and black and white prints from the same color negative, or hand-color portions of a black and white montage. To begin, all you need is one good negative.

Perhaps the family portrait might take the form of defining the primary roles that each family member enjoys. Each member can wear clothes or hold objects that reflect his or her job, hobby, or influence on the other family members.

Costumes are fun: formal wear with wigs and bare feet; scuba gear in the living room; and period costumes for a good old-fashioned family portrait—at the mall.

Technique

In most situations you'll need lots of light and a camera on a tripod. Augment the natural or bright incandescent light with a flash unit. Outdoors, the flash can be used as fill light. Indoors, flash can be bounced off a wall or ceiling.

Formal Individual Portrait

The word formal means that there should be nothing accidental about the portrait. You, the photographer, should have virtually complete control over every element of the picture: the location, lighting, background, perspective—everything. Choose the lighting you feel is appropriate for the subject and use the background to emphasize the subject and create a mood that reveals the sitter. This is not easy. The one element that you cannot control by simple choice is the reaction of the subject.

The sitter needs to feel comfortable, and this can be accomplished a number of ways. Whether you're photographing a family member, good friend, or an acquaintance, establish a relaxing mood with conversation. Choose a setting for the subject based on lighting direction and background. Keep your directions to the sitter simple; do most of the moving and adjusting of angles with the camera, not the subject. Speak of pleasant things, flatter the subject a bit, and

Amanda Perry takes full advantage of light from an overcast sky to produce plenty of details and full tonal range complete with subtle shadows. The overall softness complements skin tones and almost eliminates the need for burning and dodging in the printing stage. Overcast lighting is a favorite of portrait, fashion, and landscape photographers working with color. *Photo by Amanda Perry*

take pictures when he or she is responding to something that is fun or thoughtful. Be patient and relaxed. A rhythm will develop; enjoy it!

If you're photographing a young child or toddler, you might need some help, someone to coax a playful smile or entertain. Taking pictures right after nap time works nicely.

Technique

Seek out bright, soft, diffuse light: light coming through thin curtains or overcast conditions outdoors. If you have a choice of lenses, use a normal distance or slight telephoto lens. If you're doing a full-length portrait, use a tripod. If the picture is to be a close-in head shot, hand hold the camera so you can quickly adjust your angle. If you need a flash, cover it with a diffusion screen to soften the light. Use the fastest shutter speed possible.

The Group Portrait

There's nothing like a rowdy group to test the mettle of a rowdy photographer. Rowdy or not, the group will need direction. The group expects to be told what to do; don't disappoint them.

If the group does something special, like make music or play soccer, some planning will make it obvious. Whether you're photographing your band, doing a yearbook photo, or just memorializing the folks you play softball with, planning such a picture can be great fun. Communicate prior to the photo session; people need to know what to expect. Be clear about what they need to wear and when you need to meet.

Technique

Generally, you'll need lots of light. The trick to making good group shots is to make certain everyone is visible. Group pictures are often a situation that calls for a bird's eye view: it eliminates deep or boring backgrounds and usually allows everyone to be seen.

Portrait of a Person Working

The portrait of an individual working has many uses: photojournalism, public relations, yearbook, and resumé photography, to name a few. You can combine any of the photographic conventions you're familiar with to portray an individual at work.

Working portraits are action-oriented, even if someone is sitting at a desk. Your goal should be to tell a story that explains something important about the nature of someone's work. Does the subject make decisions that affect others? Is there an element of danger in the work? What does his or her work environment look like, and how can you most effectively relate the person to the routine?

Technique

You probably will need a flash unit. In large spaces or outdoors, the near/far conventions, using a wide-angle lens, can be very effective. If the individual uses special tools, these should be visible, even if the subject is not pictured using them.

Portraits Without People

Personal environments can be even more revealing than faces. A room, studio, office, study, workshop—each of the places where an individual spends a great deal of time with all the implements of life—says a great deal. The nature of our possessions, the way our spaces are arranged, the sparse or

What does this collection of sports footwear say about its owner? This is the kind of question posed by a portrait without people. Clear answers are not always forthcoming, but the clues are often more intriguing than the answers. Is he an athlete, a shoe salesman, an individual driven by the fashions of the day, a clever photographer, or all of the above? *Photo by Warner Saunders, Jr.*

cluttered character of our personal environs give clues to the way we structure the intimate aspects of our lives.

Technique

Close-ups of details are often useful in this aspect of portraiture. Careful, focused images of texture, with available lighting, will record a scene well set.

The Bigger Picture

As photographers we often need to refresh our vision. My own favorite method is to think in terms of the cinema and movie camera, with its wide shots, medium shots, and close-ups. It takes us in, out, along, and through the action, never resting too long on one place.

If I spend a great deal of time concerning myself with particular visual themes and images, I soon feel the need to move away from the particular to the general. Like a reader whose eyes have been glued to the pages of a good book, it's good to look away and flex our optical muscles on the larger space around us. After a moment we return to the page with renewed energy.

A challenging way to energize eyes etched with too much detail is to seek the large pattern(s) in the big picture. The goal is to seek out major elements of composition that take the form of large signs, symbols, or shapes. While your audience may not recognize the importance of these elements, for you they will be the organizational core of the image. To your eyes, these elements will be the secret subject of the photograph. There is little challenge if the symbol you search for is too obvious, too ready-made. Look for subtlety on a large, if not grand, scale.

Hidden Patterns

To the casual viewer, the bird's eye view of the two paths that meet, with the crosswalk made of large stones in the center, is an interesting view of the park and its walkways. To you, it's that and more: it's the secret triangle you searched a whole week to find. Now you must discover the hidden circle.

The images we photographers select are often built around large compositional patterns. These patterns are, in fact, compositional building blocks. You may not always be aware of the large patterns your eye settles on until long after an image is produced. The goal in finding the hidden patterns, which are not the actual subject of the picture, is to sharpen your eye to the large visual patterns that reside in the scene you're interested in. Becoming more aware of these patterns will enable you to compose (frame) your images with greater awareness.

Technique

The patterns you set out to find need not always be found in large panoramas. Scenes of every scale contain organizational elements and possibilities that you should be aware of.

Squinting at the scene before you—squeezing your eyes nearly shut—without viewing through the camera will effectively dim the light and color intensity. This dimming effect will allow you to see the large breakdown in light and dark patterns. Squint, and the scene before you is greatly simplified, dividing the scene into basic light and dark areas. Look through the camera viewer and squint. The composition will be reduced in complexity and allow you to frame the big picture and the subject within.

Whatever the scale of the picture, make certain the elements are in focus. When you are seeking specific patterns like triangles or circles, the details that merge and overlap to form the symbols you actively seek should be clear. To this end, make certain that adequate depth of field is provided for the space encompassed by the desired pattern. If the pattern you seek disappears into unfocused space, it can be lost or remain incomplete.

The Series

Photographs that are related to one another in a number of important ways can comprise a series. Certainly, they are related in terms of subject. Every subject imaginable has become the broad focus of series photography. A series of photographs accomplishes what a single photograph cannot. The series explores a subject, providing the depth and variety that only a number of images can.

A POINT OF VIEW

Just as a picture of a person is not necessarily a good portrait, a group of pictures about a particular subject is not necessarily a good series. Like the portrait, the series must reveal something special. In this case, it is a particular point of view expressed by the photographer.

In a series of photographs, point of view is expressed in a number of ways. The subject is approached in terms of several carefully selected visual themes. Different points of view depend on various approaches to time, light, and space.

Time can be portrayed in terms of immediacy or rapid pacing by allowing the blur of motion to be captured, along with tilted off-balance compositions. A point of view that speaks to stability or a timeless quality can be established by stopping action completely and carefully composing each image in a well-balanced fashion, indicating a concern for order in the world.

Space and spaces tell us much about one's point of view. Maintaining a distance from the subject of choice can indicate a detached, clinical objectivity. A constant close-up handling of spatial considerations can indicate a subjective, intimate, and perhaps emotional involvement with the subject.

Lighting can set the mood for any point of view. The harsh detail-digging light of a flash unit can speak to the hidden areas of life. Shadowy available light with broad areas of silhouette says something about mystery and danger. The bright, clarifying light of day indicates an openness that is accessible and upbeat.

When you decide on a point of view, visual common sense must prevail. Cultivate an ability to associate visual elements and symbols with your goals. You can acquire these visual sensibilities. Experience is the great teacher.

The great power of photography is that it captures images of reality, or what appears to be reality. As an unofficial project, take three identical photographs and write a reasonable, but very different, caption under each. Present the three images to three different individuals and ask each one to tell you what he or she sees. Try this when you and the other three people are together and compare the answers. Why does each individual present a different account of each photo? Perhaps it's because one picture is worth a thousand words, or at least the number of words contained in its caption (or spoken on the soundtrack). The still camera can be used to create illusions, much the same way as the motion-picture or video camera.

Some photographic series are quite long and contain hundreds of pictures. Other series are short, with just a dozen or so images. A few series are made up of many short series, like so many brief comic strips in a larger comics section of a newspaper. Most photographic series, like some motion pictures, are documentary in nature: they are pictures of moments from real events, photographic images of action as it occurs. At times the action is mundane. Sometimes we see images captured in the midst of great turmoil and violence: these are powerful images and command respect.

When a photographer works long enough, he or she begins to develop an identifiable visual style, a photographic signature made up of habits and preferences for spaces, perspectives, light, and motion, as well as subject matter. This combination of favored technique and topic forms the basis for most photographic series work.

Many photographic series come about as assignments given to photographers by photo editors. Other series are invented by the photographer. Whatever its origin, the successful series requires a plan. These photographic missions are careful investigations of a person, place, institution, or phenomenon. The subject is researched, analyzed, poked and prodded, and followed around or visited regularly. The investigation may go on for days, weeks, months, or even years. The photographer completes the series and goes on to another, never to visit the same territory in the same way again.

At times a particular series emerges from the larger body of work produced by an individual over a span of years. Slowly, over time, a photographer may discover a previously unnoticed theme emerging in his or her work. If a new theme is identified and deemed valuable, it may soon become part of a conscious collecting process. A photographer may work with more than one ongoing theme. Some themes are pursued for a lifetime.

My own experience with themes is driven by a life-long involvement with a large city. My first serious photographic efforts were influenced by the great documentary photographers Walker Evans and Eugene Atget. I spent a great deal of time photographing an old industrial section of the city that was rapidly undergoing residential development. My goal was to capture interesting images of potential historical value.

Years later my interest in documentation gave way to a search for images of a more personal nature. I began to seek out city scenes that appealed to a more emotional chord within. Over the past ten years a series has emerged that fulfills a desire to reflect on my environment. These newer images contain a very different use of formal elements such as composition, as well as different subjects.

Over time, as I made conscious decisions to shift my attention from one series to the second, something else happened. A third series of distinct images emerged from what I thought of as daily nuts-and-bolts, fun photography. In part, it came about because my usual work was accomplished with large and medium format cameras attached to tripods, a very cumbersome, calculating way of working. The new images were done with mobile small format cameras and involved people more than urban environments. The new images featured various individual figures interacting with art and architecture. The interaction between figure and art is essentially accidental and of the moment.

This recently discovered series stands in direct contrast to the very conscious and carefully planned work of my earlier years. The newer, gradually emerging series certainly relates to my training in painting and drawing, and also to a strong interest in architecture. I've come to view the recurring lone figure interacting with objects of high culture as a romantic archetype associated with art. Art with a capital A. What attitudes those individual figures share is anyone's guess.

Each of these series represents an ongoing interest that I will continue to use in my photography. My interest shifts back and forth between them, and yet there are always new subjects and themes that emerge. For me, both the planned and unplanned aspects of series photography over several decades have been exciting.

A Short Subject Series

Almost any subject can serve for a photographic series. Interesting individuals, places, institutions, and events are prime subjects. There are several basic considerations: the first is access. The subject of a series must be accessible to you over

Here a medium telephoto lens (135 mm) compresses the space in this series image. The shallow space provides proper perspective for the graphic patterns and textures of zebra and earth. This lightly humorous zoo-view contains something of the intensely two-dimensional space and fragmented views of Cubist imagery.　*Photo by Nicole Dehne*

an extended period of time. You will usually find it necessary to revisit the person, place, institution, or event. Planning a series about an event that lasts only one day and recurs but once a year may prove too condensed in time—and try your patience. If you can't see enough of the event, or if many of your images don't turn out as expected, you have to wait an entire year before you can try again.

There are at least two aspects to the question of accessibility. For example, the area where you live may have a wonderful zoo or theme park. Such institutions are wonderful subjects for a photographic series. The challenge of photographing well-known public places is to show them anew, to offer people a fresh point of view.

If you're content to make pictures of scenes and areas the general public has access to, you'll be able to return often over extended periods of time and get the pictures you want. If, however, you want behind-the-scenes pictures—scenes the public rarely sees—you'll have to request special permission. If you're able to gain access to nonpublic areas, you'll most likely be given only limited photo opportunities for short, scheduled periods of time.

If you must travel long distances to get to the places you want to serialize, be prepared to work on your project over an extended period of time. It may be a project that you work on only sporadically.

Deciding on a Point of View

Once you've decided on the subject of a series and the level of access you need, it's a good idea to spend some time sifting through the possibilities. To do this you must spend time with or at the intended subject of the series. Get the feel of it, take some pictures, but spend most of your time observing. Whatever preconceived ideas you bring to the subject may be entirely supplanted after spending time observing the real thing. For example, you might initially approach the zoo with the idea that the animal exhibits will hold the greatest possibilities for interesting images. After spending some time doing some hard looking, you may come to the conclusion that what interests you the most is the way people interact with each other and the exhibits. The initial idea was quite understandable: going to the zoo meant going to see the animals. But now, having taken in the larger scene with a greater awareness of what makes for an interesting photograph, you see a distinctively new direction.

The next phase is to concentrate on your new direction and learn how, when, and where you can position yourself to get the pictures you want. It's time to use the techniques you've acquired to insure that your images reflect your intentions. Take as many pictures as you can in various situations and locals. Process your film, make proofs, and spend time looking at the results. Determine what is successful and what is not. You need to ask yourself if you're getting close enough to the action. Are you taking advantage of various physical points of view? Do your frames look too much alike? Is there enough variety of approach? Do you need to use a flash? Is your choice of lens serving you well? By looking closely at the photographic conventions you are and are not using, you can refine your approach to the subject.

THE LOOK OF A SERIES

Subject and point of view aside, there are some basic visual considerations that can help unify a series of pictures. Many of these elements can be decided upon ahead of time. Other elements can be added in later stages of refinement.

One of the differences between photographs taken for publication and images intended for the walls of galleries and museums or book monographs, is the business of cropping images versus the use of full frame composition.

Cropping is the act of editing a picture to make it a certain proportion or to fit a space. Cropping is often done to improve the composition of the image relative to the subject. When pictures are combined with the printed word as in commercial, journalistic, and editorial publications, cropping is the rule rather than the exception. If individual cropping sends a message, perhaps it's the idea that the individual images are considered more important than any dominant point of view guiding the series. It may also be that the series was pursued over a long period of time. Various ideas have undergone changes and become more clear. Finding ways of relating individually cropped images that are part of a series is somewhat challenging, but manageable. The most common way it to standardize matting, mounting, and framing (the use of picture frames), making certain that the outside dimensions of mats and frames are the same.

Full-Frame Images

The technique of using full-frame images insures that all of the images of a series will be the same proportion and, later, the same print size. This method of unifying images begins when the photographer decides to accept everything in the frame of the camera's viewer. Thus, when the pictures are taken, great effort goes into framing the image, or carefully composing the subject in strict conformity with the proportions of the film format. The photographer does this having decided that there will be little or no cropping later on.

Many photographers print their images using a negative carrier with an oversized opening for the negative. Such a carrier allows light to surround the projected image, producing a black line of light around the entire print. The thickness of the line is controlled by the printing easel. The inner edge of black line surrounding the print is somewhat irregular and, aside from providing a black linear frame, it clearly denotes a photograph that was conceived as a full frame image.

Refining the Series

Refinements in the presentation of a series include the manner in which the work is printed. As a series takes shape and test prints are produced, the photographer must decide many questions: how large to print the images; the most suitable overall print contrast; whether the images are to be toned; and finally how they might be presented in the home, gallery, book, or album.

Print size is important. Large prints are easily seen from a distance and present an undeniable boldness. Large prints confront the viewer with photographic information that is usually seen on a much smaller scale in books, magazines, and photo albums. Large prints take on the formidable character of posters and paintings.

A series of photographs can make a strong impression even when they are small, or *because* they are small. The subject of the series may have a strong, intimate quality, an aura that is more effectively shared if the viewer is brought close to the image, as we might be when viewing a personal album. A prime example of suitably small images would be a series of portraits using large format negatives. A contact print of a 4 × 5 or 5 × 7–inch negative would represent the greatest possible detail in a very small exhibition format. The combination of small print and extreme detail would complement portraits that appeared very personal in nature—personal in the sense that they are not intended for any other purpose than as a record of friends or family.

Most photographs intended for public viewing are easier to see when printed large. Most series benefit from the larger scale. Some of the most dramatic public presentations have been of series pictures, such as full-face portraits, that are enlarged to proportions equal to the size of household walls. Making what is usually intimate in size giant in nature represents a great reversal in terms of presentation and expectation. The effects are dramatic.

The overall print contrast of a series is an important ingredient in the presentation of your point of view. High-contrast images can appear harsh and bold. Low-contrast prints have a softness that complements a gentle nature. Average contrast is somewhat neutral, accommodating a range of emotional energy. If a particular contrast treatment doesn't suggest itself immediately, make some test prints using series images that appear to represent extremes of mood and boldness. Make some high-, normal-, and low-contrast prints of each and live with them for a time. Keep the images where you can see them and react to them abruptly in passing. After awhile, you'll be able to make a decision.

Toning black and white prints adds a protective coating to the silver that can also change the contrast and color of the print. Contrast and color provide strong mood enhancement and may add an element of cohesion to your series. Gold toning, brown toning, sepia, and selenium toning are among the toning treatments most commonly used in photography. If you decide to investigate the use of toners, be sure to observe prescribed safety precautions.

HAND-COLORING IMAGES

When you hand color a series of photographs, be careful to insure consistent color and application technique. The same type and combination of coloring materials should be used on each photo of the same series.

Hand coloring can appear subtle or bold. Styles of hand coloring can seem more individual in nature than any purely chemical or photographic technique, such as toning or the use of a particular lens. Before you begin hand coloring a photo series, you should work out the style of application. In other words, practice different styles first, and *then* color the final prints. For details on suggested materials, see chapter 9.

SUGGESTED TOPICS FOR SHORT SERIES

Home Life

It might seem corny or too familiar, but photographing your home life invites exploration. Surely, you have some thoughts on how to characterize your home life and the people you live with. The difference between home life and the usual album images is the difference between everyday activity and special occasions. We cover the big events, but everyday rituals get lost. Take the time to record everyone doing his or her characteristic, everyday activities. In 10, 20, or 30 years you'll look at pictures of "home" and see that you captured a wonderful visual record.

The Band

The band can be an actual group of musicians or a euphemism for any group that does something together. Perhaps the most interesting thing about any group is what it does behind the scenes, while traveling, setting up, rehearsing, arguing about the music, buying new or used equipment, relaxing, and then, appearing in performance.

A Favorite Institution

Places can be complex and offer much to many people. Schools, museums, parks, city halls, hospitals, military bases— one or even all of these institutions can hold intense personal meaning for any of us. The experiences that we may associate with a particular institution may not be altogether pleasant, but pleasure is not always the most important element in a story. The older you are the more institutions and stories you have to choose from. Some institutions are fairly open and offer easy access. Some, like hospitals and military bases, are

This image from a short series about a rock band is illuminated by electronic flash during a rehearsal. The flash selects bright reflective surfaces that form stark patterns and shapes. Live shows present photographers with interesting and challenging lighting situations. Flash represents one possible lighting solution, but it rarely captures the special lighting effects that form an integral part of the performance atmosphere. Extremely sensitive film will provide a flexible solution when you are dealing with available light. *Photo by Sara Beugen*

essentially closed affairs, and yet you'd be surprised at the openness that a direct, polite request for access can lead to.

Illustrate a Story

We many not have the inclination to invent visual stories, but illustrating poetry, short stories, or even a favorite novel can provide a dramatic interplay between literary and photographic imagery. Most illustration for stories and novels has been crafted by those who draw and paint. Photography has often been considered too "real" to illustrate works of fiction. The challenge is to provide a meaningful photographic illustration that leaves room for the reader's imagination.

Public Service Message

Create a series of public service messages designed to make a point. Public service messages attempt to educate us, warn us, entreat us to do something, encourage us to take some action. Most such messages are related to health and safety threats. Some ask us to join a cause to take action that favors the environment. The photographic challenge is to create an image that grabs the viewer's attention and stirs the imagination! Most such messages are accompanied by words. Try to create a visual message that doesn't rely on words.

Other Artists, New Ideas

The history of art is filled with accounts of how the masters went about learning their craft. A strong recurring message runs through these accounts like a rainbow in the mist. Good artists are good students. Great artists are great students. No source of ideas is left unexamined. Everything is seen, everyone is heard, no detail is ignored. The ideas, methods, and techniques of others are borrowed, copied, emulated, and used until they are understood. Above all, the desire to attain complete originality is set aside in favor of working hard at playing with ideas. You must be always collecting ideas. Only then will you begin to put together your own unique set of them.

It's clear that creativity is anything but narrow. We must look for ideas, inspiration, guidance, and even heroes wherever we can find them. Science, art, politics, music, literature, drama—everywhere. We can begin by seeing where it is we want to go.

Those who wish to write read the works of great authors. Those who wish to make great photographs look at the work of great photographers. Choosing the influences that shape your vision is one of the great shopping trips of life. With a little luck and effort the journey will last a lifetime.

Additional Reading

The Americans by Robert Frank. An Aperture Book, Museum of Modern Art edition, 1969.

Suburbia by Bill Owens. Straight Arrow Books, 1973.

11 | Presenting and Storing Your Photographs

This crowded image suggests many ways and means available to conserve and present your photographs. Handling photographs requires care. The purpose of a photograph should determine how you present it. Cropping and mounting images, cutting mats and buying frames, choosing an album or portfolio—it all adds up to the necessary final touch.

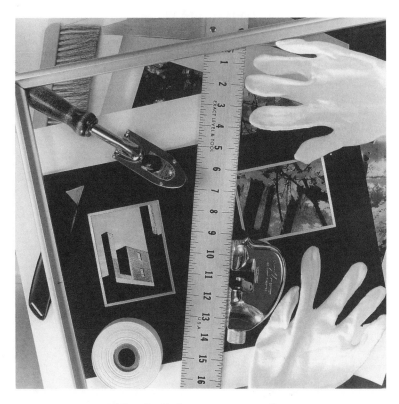

Finishing Touches

N ewly processed photographs are ready for a wide range of creative finishing touches that can greatly enhance the viewing experience. The manner in which pictures are displayed can insure the ultimate appreciation of ideas and images.

Finishing touches include spotting and limited forms of retouching. These are often necessary to eliminate flaws resulting from damage to negatives and to provide color for black and white processing.

Images that are intended for public display should be large enough for easy viewing. Generally, images are mounted or matted, placed behind protective glass, and framed. Some photographs are meant for occasional viewing, such as pictures in a family album or special collections of personal photographs placed in archival collection boxes. Other photographs are put in presentation portfolios, suitable for easy carrying and portable presentation.

The business of storing and preserving photographic images begins with the processing of negatives and prints. The term archival refers to the many ways that we can go about the task of preserving photographic images. To be involved in archival processing, presentation, and storage means to employ processes, methods, and materials that contribute to the long-term preservation of photographs.

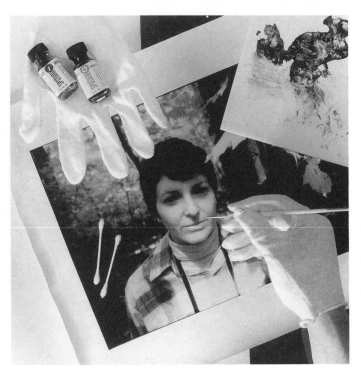

Included in the aesthetics of the photographic process is the spotting of color and black and white photos. Cotton editing gloves, a spotting brush, photo dyes, a white mixing palette, and cotton swabs are essentials.

Spotting Your Pictures

Photographic prints often show the ravages of dust, scratches, finger-prints, and other blemishes acquired during processing and printing. White spots, scratches, and blotches, if small enough, can be spotted away. Large blemishes must undergo retouching of various sorts.

Spotting entails the use of dyes on black and white, as well as color negatives and prints. Most spotting is performed on prints and at times on large format negatives.

The dyes for black and white materials are mixed with water to produce the full scale of gray tones. The spotting dyes are applied with small, fine-point brushes. The dyes are formulated to soak into the emulsion of prints and negatives. The dye will not work on paper where the emulsion has been scratched away. Spotting dye colors are purchased individually or in sets. The dyes can be mixed in prescribed proportions to match the color of any black and white paper. Repeated application of a mixture of dye and water will gradually darken a spot, matching the area of black or gray surrounding it. When this is done carefully, little or no trace of a blemish will remain.

It is common to spot pinhole positives and negatives. If a negative has a white blemish, a bit of black ink or marker will serve to block light and produce a blemish-free positive.

Special dyes for spotting color prints and color negatives are used in much the same as those for black materials, except that mixing and matching colors is also required.

Spotting away blemishes on a good print is time well spent. Dust spots or scratches will detract from the careful illusion of an image. Any flaw that can be fixed shouldn't prevent the enjoyment of a beautiful image.

Spotting requires a spotting brush (I recommend 00005; it's the finest point), some dye to match your paper, white dish or tile to mix a pallet of tones, and some cotton swabs to soak up excess water and dye.

Mounting Photographs

Mounting a picture or photograph provides a flat surface for easy viewing. Mounts are usually larger that the actual image, providing a neutral boarder area around the entire picture, isolating the image from the surrounding colors and textures of a wall or display case.

Pictures can be mounted in albums or on paper board. Albums can hold photographs between sheets of clear plastic, or fasten them by paper or plastic mounting corners (triangular pockets that hold the corners of prints). Photographs can also be mounted on flat boards with the aid of adhesive materials. Some adhesives are liquids sprayed onto photos and boards and then joined by contact ("wet mounting"). Solid, dry adhesive sheets, activated by heat are also used to mount prints ("dry mounting"). Most mounting processes are considered permanent because efforts to undo the process can result in damage to the print. Processes using corner mounts or tape hinges are considered to be temporary and allow prints to be removed without damage. All of these mounting methods can be used with picture mats.

Mounting pictures is the easiest and least expensive way to provide flat, attractive support for pictures that are to be framed or placed in storage boxes for occasional viewing. Dry mounting with heat-activated tissue is the method most often used by commercial photo finishers and students.

MOUNTING COLOR AND RESIN-COATED PRINTS

Excessive heat will damage color prints and resin-coated paper. Use dry mount tissue for color and RC paper. This material will adhere at lower temperatures than tissue made for prints on fiber-based papers.

MOUNTING HAND-COLORED IMAGES

If hand-colored images are to be mounted, the images should be colored after mounting is completed. In addition, hand-colored images should be placed in a museum-style mat. This will reduce the likelihood of damage to coloring agents by touching glass used in framing.

Matting Photographs

Simple mats, or window mats, are essentially cardboard frames—cardboard sheets with a cutout section that allows the image area of a photograph to show through. A more substantial type, called a museum mat, has a front window section and a hinged backing piece. The photograph is placed between the two, attached to the backing, and visible through the front window mat.

Museum mats allow photographs to be safely stored in boxes or placed in picture frames. The window section of the mat provides an air space between the photograph and the glass sheet that usually covers framed prints. Museum mats can also be covered with glass and attached to walls, or panels, with L hooks. No frame is required.

Most museum mats allow photographs to be attached to the backing sheet without the use of permanent adhesives. Paper or linen tape hinges or corner mounts secure the print to the back of the mat. Museum matting is the preferred method for storing and framing photographs because it offers protection, allows the image to be easily viewed, and does not damage the print. Prints can be removed from the mat at any time, with no wear and tear.

Mats with multiple windows can be cut to accommodate several photographs. Matting several pictures under one mat is an effective way of relating photos in a series. Mats can also be cut from actual photo images that have been mounted on cardboard, lending a photo montage look to the presentation of images.

Mats are usually cut by hand using a variety of mat-cutting tools. These tools allow the window section of the mat to be cut with a beveled or angled edge to prevent any shadow from being cast on the print. The beveled edge also offers a smooth visual transition from window mat to picture. Small mats can be cut using blades mounted on inexpensive sled-like holders that are pushed along a straight edge or T-square. Large mats are easily cut using blade holders attached to rails. Large mat cutters are usually quite expensive. Museum mats require more material than mounting, but offer the greatest protection for prints and drawings.

Small, decorative mats can often be purchased from photo stores, some of which deal in used photo equipment. Some of their resale stock comes from portrait studios and includes the type of mat commonly used for delivering commercial portraits. These inexpensive mats make handy display and storage units for small photos, including pinhole camera images.

Picture Albums and Portfolios

Today there are a great variety of picture albums and portfolios for storing and exhibiting photographs. Preparing an album or portfolio requires care and precision. Pictures should be easily viewed and protected at the same time. Designing special albums with thin picture mats, or mats with multiple windows for the display of several photos in a single mat, is one way of providing albums or portfolios with a special look.

Archival Materials

Interest in preserving photographic images has increased greatly in recent years. To accommodate this widespread interest, archival processes and materials are more readily available. Archival processing entails the proper fixing of images and the thorough elimination of processing chemicals from negatives and prints. It also extends to the materials used to store and present pictures. Archival materials are those that are free of substances that harm paper and light-sensitive emulsions. Mounting and matting materials, storage boxes, and portfolios—all materials that negatives and prints come in contact with—are available in archival form. Becoming familiar with the long-term advantages of archival processing and materials is the best way to conserve your photographic images.

Additional Reading

Caring for Photographs: Display, Storage, Restoration. Life Library of Photography, Time-life Books, 1972.

Light Impressions Archival Supplies Catalog. 439 Monroe Ave., Rochester, New York 14607-3717.

Index

ZIGGURAT BOOKS
FROM CHICAGO REVIEW PRESS

Ziggurat A temple of the ancient Assyrians and Babylonians, having the form of a terraced pyramid of successively receding stories. Assyrian *ziqquratu*, summit, mountain top, from *zaqaru*, to be high.   —*American Heritage Dictionary of the English Language*

Ziggurat Books are project books for talented young people of middle and high school age, ten or eleven and up. Many are science or technology oriented; others involve literature or the fine and applied arts. All emphasize a hands-on, experimental approach to adult disciplines such as physics, astronomy, the graphic arts, architecture, and creative writing.

Ziggurat Books give students a taste of a wide variety of adult professions. They provide innovative, challenging material for science and art fairs, class and individual school projects. Most important, they enable young people to explore their talents as they experience the effort and the excitement of creative work.

Art of Construction:
Projects and Principles for
Beginning Engineers and Architects
by Mario Salvadori
ISBN 1-55652-080-8
144 pages, paper, $9.95

The Art of the Handmade Book:
Designing, Decorating, and
Binding One-of-a-Kind Books
by Flora Fennimore
ISBN 1-55652-146-4
144 pages, paper, $11.95

Exploring the Sky: Projects for
Beginning Astronomers
Revised Edition
by Richard Moeschl
ISBN 1-55652-160-X
320 pages, paper, $14.95

Faraday's Chemical History of a Candle:
Twenty-Two Experiments
and Six Classic Lectures
by Michael Faraday
ISBN 1-55652-035-2
136 pages, paper, $9.95

Real Toads in Imaginary Gardens:
Suggestions and Starting Points for
Young Creative Writers
by Stephen Phillip Policoff
and Jeffrey Skinner
ISBN 1-55652-137-5
192 pages, paper, $11.95

The Spark in the Stone: Skills and Projects
from the Native American Tradition
by Peter Goodchild
ISBN 1-55652-102-2
132 pages, paper, $11.95

These books are available through your local bookstore or directly from **Independent Publishers Group, 814 North Franklin Street, Chicago, Illinois, 60610, 1-800-888-4741.** Visa and MasterCard accepted.